PLANETARY
APOTHECARY

STEPHANIE GAILING

planetary
apothecary

an astrological approach to
health and wellness

CROSSING PRESS
Berkeley | Toronto

To everyone who shares their love and wisdom with the world

Crossing Press
an imprint of Ten Speed Press
PO Box 7123
Berkeley, California 94707
www.tenspeed.com

Distributed in Australia by Simon and Schuster Australia, in Canada by Ten Speed Press Canada, in New Zealand by Southern Publishers Group, in South Africa by Real Books, and in the United Kingdom and Europe by Publishers Group UK.

Cover and text design by Betsy Stromberg

Library of Congress Cataloging-in-Publication Data

Gailing, Stephanie.
  Planetary apothecary : an astrological approach to health and wellness / Stephanie Gailing.
       p. cm.
  Includes bibliographical references and index.
  Summary: "A guide to medical astrology that provides health and wellness therapies, holistic remedies, and self-care tips for each sign of the zodiac"
—Provided by publisher.
  ISBN-13: 978-1-58091-191-7
  ISBN-10: 1-58091-191-9
  1. Medical astrology. I. Title.

  BF1718.G26 2009
  133.5′861—dc22

Printed in China
First printing, 2009

1 2 3 4 5 6 7 8 9 10 — 13 12 11 10 09

CONTENTS

ACKNOWLEDGMENTS

Planetary Apothecary has been my labor of love. And yet it would not have been possible without the gracious and kind individuals who shared their wisdom, insight, and inspiration with me and to whom I am deeply grateful:

★ My dear family and friends, for their outpouring of love and support

★ My grandfather, Abe Ginsburg, for always encouraging me to write and share my ideas with the world

★ Sophie, Maeve, and Ari, for being beacons of light

★ Alexander Carrillo, for his brilliant mind filled with never-ending creative ideas, incredibly astute editing skills, and unconditional support

★ Aimee Hartstein, who served as a compassionate and instructive sounding board for me during the writing of this book

★ Ingrid Emerick, editing consultant extraordinaire, for her vision and uncanny ability to help me refine my ideas and the words used to express them

★ Melina Meza, for inspiring my creativity as well as for her valuable contributions to the yoga poses sections

★ Laurie Baum, for her dedicated and intuitive astrological guidance

★ George Mateljan, Buck Levin, and Tenji Cowan, for sharing their passion for nutrition and whole foods with me

★ My friends and colleagues who read and reviewed the manuscript and who provided me with valuable feedback

★ Everyone at Crossing Press who helped to transform my manuscript into the book you are holding in your hands today, including acquiring editor Julie Bennett, for believing in the book; editor Brie Mazurek, for her on-point insights and support; designer Betsy Stromberg, for designing a beautiful book; and copy editor Laura Quilling and proofreader Mike Ashby, for their attention to detail

★ And finally, to all the astrologers and health-care practitioners, past and present, whose contributions to the healing arts inspire and enable us to more readily pursue a life of conscious well-being

INTRODUCTION

YEARS AGO, TO MY DELIGHT, I discovered that there was a healing art that combined two of my greatest passions: natural health and astrology. Always looking for ways to inspire people to achieve their optimal well-being, I decided to write *Planetary Apothecary* to bring this elegant, time-honored healing tradition—known as *medical astrology*—to modern-day readers who are looking to further enhance their health.

While many people turn to astrology to garner insights into relationships, career, and unfolding life events, your planetary profile can also guide the way you approach personal wellness. It can help you identify natural remedies and healing techniques that are best suited for your unique temperament and individual health needs.

A stellar approach to evaluating health and proposing therapies to foster vitality, medical astrology has a long and legendary past: It was documented by ancient Greek scholars, taught in medieval medical schools, and practiced by Renaissance physicians. Up until the early twentieth century, many doctors employed its observations alongside other methods of treatment. The study of the stars was so integral to the work of many healers that none other than the father of modern medicine, Hippocrates himself, was reported as saying, "He who does not understand astrology is not a doctor but a fool." Today you will find astrology professionals and health-care practitioners worldwide studying, and relying on, this graceful method of insight to offer clients an instructive way to approach their health-care needs.

At the heart of medical astrology is the tenet "As above, so below," reflecting the long-held belief in the connection between the celestial bodies and our own bodies. The zodiac signs and their ruling planets are associated with various body parts, physiological functions, and emotional tendencies (with some areas of health cogoverned by more than one astrological signifier). In addition, the signs and planets have alliances with different members of the plant, mineral, and animal kingdoms. For example, Aries is the first sign in the zodiac and is associated with the head, while Pisces is the last sign and is associated with the feet. Leo, ruled by the Sun, has an affinity for yellow flowers such as sunflower and chamomile, while Taurus, governed by feminine Venus, has a kinship with trees that bear sweet fruits such as peaches and plums.

Practitioners who use medical astrology utilize the information gleaned from their clients' personalized astrology charts to offer them custom-designed wellness solutions. They employ these insights as a tool to assess health strengths and weaknesses, determine the best remedies and therapies, suggest the timing of proposed treatments, and evaluate underlying psycho-emotional patterns that may stand in the way of healing. They don't use this astrologically derived information as the sole means of diagnosis and treatment, but rather as a complement to traditional methods of health-care investigation and advice.

Even if you never consult with a medical astrologer, you can still integrate some of this healing art's fundamentals into your wellness regimen by using *Planetary Apothecary* as your guide. In this book, I take the classical wisdom of medical astrology and apply it to our modern-day health-care needs. As a foundation, I draw on the knowledge inherent in the traditional associations between "as above" (the planets and zodiacal constellations) and "so below" (ourselves and the healing gifts of nature, including foods, herbs, and flowers) as delineated by the ancient masters. With this time-honored tradition in mind, I also offer insights into contemporary healing activities popular today—such as spa and wellness therapies, relaxation practices, and yoga poses—matching their benefits to the needs of those born under the different astrological signs. Combined with the extensive information on the tendencies and temperaments of each sign, this knowledge will allow you to more readily navigate the maze of healthy foods, natural remedies, and self-care treatments available today, choosing those that are more aligned with your disposition, constitution, and health needs.

how to use this book

Planetary Apothecary is divided into twelve chapters—one dedicated to each of the zodiac signs. Each chapter includes individualized wellness profiles as well as holistic health approaches targeted for each of the astrological personalities and temperaments.

To gain insights into your personal health, first read through the chapter on your Sun sign. Your *Sun sign* represents your vitality and the essence of who you are. It is the spark that energizes your being and therefore a significant factor in understanding your personalized wellness needs.

Next, if you know your Ascendant and Moon signs, read through those chapters as well, as these astrological signatures represent other important facets of your overall health picture. Your *Ascendant sign* (often referred to as the *Rising sign*) symbolizes the way that you present yourself to the world and describes characteristics of your physical body, making it an important signifier of your health. Your *Moon sign* embodies your emotional being and can give you clues as to which health-care approaches you may find particularly nurturing, both for physical health as well as emotional well-being.

If you don't know your Ascendant or Moon signs, don't worry; reading your Sun sign chapter will provide you with in-depth wellness insights. But if you're curious to know what they are, it's easy enough to find out. These astrological positions are calculated according to the day, time, and place you were born; with this simple information, you can discover your Ascendant and Moon signs—as well as other information specific to your horoscope—by having a website astrology service or astrologer cast your personalized chart (check the Resources section at the end of the book for astrology websites and for ways to find astrologers).

Each chapter provides in-depth information and practical tips that will help you make lifestyle choices that best support your individual needs. You'll learn more about your astrological health portrait as well as the treatments, activities, and remedies that can bolster your optimal well-being.

Every chapter opens by exploring the fundamentals of that particular astrological sign. In addition to general characteristics, it also covers information about your sign's symbol, planetary ruler, element, and quality, all of which can provide further understanding of your unique astrological temperament. It also features the following ten sections:

Personal Health Profile

Your personal health profile gives you insights into the attitudes that shape your sign's approach to wellness. It provides a glimpse into innate tendencies and habits that affect your sign's unique well-being and the areas of self-care to which you may be especially attracted.

Areas of Health Focus

In medical astrology, different parts of the body are associated with each of the twelve signs, as are different psychological propensities that may contribute to feelings of *dis*-ease. Each chapter highlights practical approaches for bolstering these areas of health.

Healthy Eating Tips

Natives of each sign have different personalities, which can lead to dietary habits that either support or stand in the way of optimal health. This section provides healthy eating tips that are geared toward your unique temperament and that can help you boost your overall healthfulness.

Health-Supporting Foods

Certain foods are particularly beneficial for certain signs. Find the foods that are ruled by your sign and/or help address particular health concerns specific to your individual astrological profile.

Spa and Wellness Therapies

Spa and wellness therapies include bodywork (such as massage), rejuvenating treatments (such as herbal wraps), complementary practices (such as acupuncture), and mind-body techniques (such as biofeedback). Each of these natural-health treatments— available at spas and from individual health-care practitioners—has its own style and benefits; as such, some are better matched to the personalities and health characteristics of the different signs. Discover the best spa and wellness therapies to foster your personal health and beauty.

Relaxation Practices

Distinct from spa and wellness therapies, relaxation practices are self-directed activities that you can do on your own. From journaling to gardening to meditation and more, numerous enjoyable activities can reduce stress and foster relaxation. As each fulfills a different need and is attuned to a distinct temperament, certain ones are more in sync with particular zodiac signs.

Yoga Poses

Yoga provides a holistic approach to exercise that increases physical strength and flexibility while calming the mind and inspiring the spirit. While there are hundreds of yoga poses (also known as asanas) that can benefit general well-being, certain poses target particular body parts or health concerns and therefore are more aligned with specific astrological signs. Investigate the poses that can best meet your needs.

Aromatherapy

Aromatherapy is a therapeutic art that uses the aromatic essences of plants—their flowers, fruits, leaves, and wood—to foster well-being. Use the healing fragrances of these essential oils in baths and massage oils, as perfumes, or to scent a room (please note that essential oils should not be used internally). With their distinctive qualities, as well as the astrological correspondence between plants and planets, it makes sense that different scents are especially suited for different zodiacal signs. Learn which essential oils can enhance your individual well-being.

Natural Remedies

Natural remedies—such as dietary supplements, herbs, and homeopathics—have become an important part of many people's wellness regimens. Different remedies are valuable for specific zodiac-related health conditions. In addition, in medical astrology the various planets and signs have established correspondences with the many plants and nutrients that comprise different natural remedies. In this section, discover those that may be beneficial for natives of your sign.

✺ Flower Essences

These natural elixirs, made from flower-infused water, work energetically to restore mental and emotional balance. Flower essences can help you let go of certain habits and perspectives that stand in your way of whole health. While the stress-relieving Rescue Remedy is the most well-known, there are scores of individual flower essences that can be used therapeutically. Various flower essences accord with distinct psycho-emotional constitutions and, as such, address the unique temperaments associated with each of the twelve signs. Discover which essences are targeted for the inherent disposition represented by your astrological sign.

AS YOU JOURNEY THROUGH *Planetary Apothecary,* you'll not only explore what foods, natural remedies, and activities are most supportive of the characteristics of your sign but also *why* they are beneficial. Really understanding your individual needs, both physical and emotional, is vital to living a healthy and balanced life. If you know what makes you tick, it follows that you will have an easier time integrating those habits and choices into your routine. After all, health is not just something measured by the absence of illness or discomfort but by the vitality that is experienced when you live in sync with your true nature. It is my hope that *Planetary Apothecary* helps you create and sustain unique and effective wellness practices that will greatly improve the quality of your life.

While the planets may seem far away, with the information we can glean from them, thanks to medical astrology, wellness is much closer than we think.

aries

SUN IN ARIES ★ March 21–April 19

CHARACTERISTICS ★ Willful / Enterprising / Assertive / Pioneering / Energetic / Impulsive / Impatient / Brave / Carefree / Hot-tempered / Direct / Individualistic

SYMBOL ★ The *Ram*, an animal known for its strength, will, and competitive nature. In mythological and cultural traditions, the Ram is a symbol of power, new beginnings, and renewal.

PLANETARY RULER ★ *Mars*, often called the "Red Planet" in reference to its color. Mars was the Roman god of war and fertility, known for his ability to fight, defend, and protect. His counterpart in Greek mythology was Ares. In astrology, Mars represents desire, courage, self-initiation, and a call to action.

ELEMENT ★ *Fire*, characterized by the dynamic energy of inspiration, enthusiasm, and passion. It is transformative, kinetic, and action oriented.

QUALITY ★ *Cardinal*, which represents the initiation of the creative cycle. It reflects ambition, enterprise, speed, and a self-starting force that propels energy into the world.

Ariens are blessed with great vitality. After all, yours is the sign of spring, the season that reflects the burgeoning of new life. Your tremendous energy reserves and fiery spirit make you well poised for experiencing abundant health and longevity.

When you do get sick, you take it seriously and, like a true Ram, face the situation head-on. For an Arien, illness becomes yet another thing to conquer, eliciting your inner warrior. And conquer it you must, since you want to return quickly to the playing field of life. Sitting on the sidelines is unbearable for your feisty spirit.

While assertive Ariens are often armed with clear strategies to reach their wellness goals, they are sometimes short on the patience required to see them through. As with all you take on, you like to see immediate results. If you don't get that near-instant gratification from your well-intentioned actions, you may feel tempted to abandon even your best-laid plans.

One way to stay the course is to set smaller, easier-to-accomplish goals. For example, don't set a hard-to-achieve target of losing four pounds in one week; instead shoot for one to two pounds, a mark that you can more readily accomplish week after week. This strategy for achieving your wellness goals will honor your action-oriented nature while helping to temper your impatience, bringing optimal health more immediately within your grasp.

As Ariens are pioneers, you will likely try many wellness activities and natural remedies before others even hear of them. The ones that best serve you are those that honor your active nature. Sitting passively is not for you. You want to be involved and engaged. This is one of the reasons that Ariens rarely have problems committing to an exercise program, a very important pillar of a healthy lifestyle.

When a health issue calls for some outside assistance, it's important to find a health-care practitioner who involves you directly in decision making since, as in many areas of your life, it's important for you to feel like you are in charge. Because, to an Arien, there's no point in not getting to the point, your ideal medical specialists are straightforward communicators who display candor and honesty, qualities that the Ram appreciates.

 ## AREAS OF HEALTH FOCUS

Each zodiac sign is associated with certain parts of the body. These may be inherent areas of vulnerability, but when attended to, they can become areas of strength. The parts of the body associated with Aries include the following:

★ The **head** and **brain**, which control physical and mental activities

★ The **muscular system**, which gives you strength

★ The **blood**, which carries energizing oxygen to the muscles and all of the body's organs

★ The **adrenal glands**, which govern the stress response and the fight-or-flight mechanism

Your Arien pioneering spirit, strong will, and formidable instincts are some of the resources you can use when facing any health challenge.

Stay Ahead of Headaches

Aries rules the head and brain, which unfortunately also means that many Rams are vulnerable to headaches, some powerful enough to stop you right in your tracks. Taking time to relax, in whatever way best suits your Arien on-the-go nature, is important when you get a headache (and for preventing them in the first place). Additionally, keep tabs on your diet to see if particular foods lead to a throbbing noggin; for example, many migraine sufferers are sensitive to aged cheese, sour cream, red wine, and chocolate. And don't forget to keep your water intake flowing throughout your busy day, as dehydration is a leading cause of headaches.

Prevent Strains and Sprains

Your ruling planet, Mars, governs the muscular system, which is integral to all things Arien (such as movement and action). To protect your muscles, try to override your impetuous instincts long enough to stretch and warm up before you dive into your exercise routine. If you find that you're prone to muscle cramps, consider increasing your intake of magnesium-rich foods such as green vegetables, seeds, and fish. With Aries ruling the head, you may be prone to carrying some of your stress in your facial and jaw muscles; when you go for a massage, make sure the therapist works on this area to release any pent-up tension. And as you zip from one activity to the next, be careful to avoid accidental mishaps that can result in strains, sprains, and bruises.

Support Your Adrenal Glands

Ariens are always on alert, ready to respond to the situation at hand without even batting an eye. Your warrior fight-or-flight instinct is well honed and can prove helpful in times of crisis. Yet, if your nervous system is constantly geared up for battle, it may also tax your energy reserves, depleting your adrenal glands and impacting your long-term ability to effectively respond to stress. Luckily, you can be proactive on the nutrition front and boost your adrenals by curbing excess caffeine intake and ensuring that your diet features adequate amounts of vitamin B5–rich foods, such as yogurt, sunflower seeds, mushrooms, and corn.

Rest and Recuperate

Ariens are on the go from the get-go. Your pep and verve get you moving and keep you moving long after others have called it a day. Your energetic nature knows no bounds, which can be a boon when you're healthy but a challenge when you're not. Since you're used to being on the move, taking the time to rest and recuperate is not your forte. Yet doing so is often the best strategy to help you quickly shore up your energy reserves, putting you back on the fast track to vibrant health with all of your vitality in tow.

 # HEALTHY EATING TIPS

While Ariens are often on the run, it's important to take the time to stop (even if for a moment) to nourish yourself with health-promoting foods that can kindle your energy and vitality.

Take Time to Eat Breakfast

Out of the gate running, Ariens like to avoid obstacles that seem to slow them down. For many Ariens, one such perceived barrier to getting the day under way is eating breakfast. Yet it's no understatement that breakfast can be the most important meal of the day, and even a quick one can provide you with the lasting energy you need to power through your bustling schedule.

★ A hard-boiled egg, whole-wheat crackers and cheese, or muesli mixed with raisins and nuts are a few ideas for quick and energizing morning meals. If you don't have time to eat at home, you can always brown-bag it to work or school.

Cool It

Fire-sign Ariens often crave foods that are spicy and hot. While piquant foods can fan your inner flames, an overabundance of heat, according to Ayurvedic traditions, may cause rashes and irritability. When it comes to spicy foods, the key is moderation—not a concept that comes easily to Ariens, but one that is important to practice.

★ You can balance out the heat by enjoying cooling foods such as sweet fruit, basmati rice, sprouts, and watery vegetables (including lettuce and cucumber). In Ayurvedic nutrition, poultry is considered more cooling than red meat; the latter is thought to aggravate the fiery constitution to which an Arien may be prone. If you feel overheated between meals, mint tea or filtered water can help cool you down.

Iron Out Your Diet

Aries governs the blood as well as the mineral iron. For optimal health, you'll want to make sure your diet includes adequate supplies of this nutrient, which functions to oxygenate your blood and muscles, topping off your energy reserves. While meat is a ready source of iron, you can also get your fix of this important mineral via a cornucopia of plant-based foods.

★ Vegetarian foods that will help you meet your iron goals include spinach, chard, pumpkin seeds, beans, and lentils. If you want a sweetener that will energize you with its iron content, try blackstrap molasses.

 HEALTH-SUPPORTING FOODS

Fruits, vegetables, sprouts, and other foods that capture the energy of spring can help your vitality to bloom. Foods associated with your planetary ruler, Mars, can also be health-promoting additions to an Arien's diet.

Sprouts

Just like the sign of Aries, sprouts represent the initial stages of growth, when all that can exist first bursts onto the scene, declaring itself to the world. Sprouts contain concentrated amounts of nutrients and contribute to a sense of well-being. In addition to popular alfalfa sprouts, look for those made from mung beans and lentils as well as broccoli, sunflower, and radish seeds.

★ Top a sandwich or green salad with your favorite sprouts. Look for bread made from sprouted grains. Not only does sprouted bread taste great, but many people claim that it is easier to digest. Sprouts are simple to grow at home and require a minimal investment of time and money.

Garlic

Garlic has long been associated with your planetary ruler, Mars. Like the mythic Mars, garlic is a warrior; its ability to fight off bacteria and viruses has been well documented. It is also very good for circulatory health, reducing cholesterol and triglyceride levels as well as platelet stickiness.

★ No matter what cuisine you favor, you're bound to find recipes that include garlic since it is a prized ingredient in many cultures. To maximize its health benefits, let garlic sit for five minutes after you chop it and before you add it to a recipe. This process allows for greater production of allicin, one of its health-empowering phytonutrients.

Red Foods

Red is associated with Aries: it's the color of your element, fire, as well as the brilliant hue that emanates from Mars. So why not enjoy a host of nutrient-rich red foods? For example, beets are rich in appetite-satisfying fiber, tomatoes are filled with heart-healthy lycopene, and cayenne peppers contain the natural pain-relieving capsaicin.

★ Roast whole beets in the oven for a deliciously sweet side dish, or add raw beets to a red leaf salad. Since fat increases lycopene absorption, add some extra virgin olive oil to recipes that include tomatoes. Make salsa even redder by adding cayenne pepper (but only a pinch so you don't overheat).

SPA AND WELLNESS THERAPIES

While it may be challenging for an Arien to stop long enough to enjoy a spa and wellness therapy, doing so every now and again can be very valuable for your health.

Shirodhara

Shirodhara is an Ayurvedic healing treatment focused on the Aries-ruled head. Warm herb-infused sesame oil is gently poured onto the center of your forehead. The slow-flowing oil cascades onto your scalp and neck, which then receive an invigorating massage. This therapy induces deep relaxation and is used to treat headaches, sinusitis, and allergies. *Shirodhara* is also said to foster mental clarity by synchronizing the brain's alpha waves.

★ *Shirodhara* is performed in many spas as well as in the offices of Ayurvedic health-care practitioners. The herbs included in the oil treatment are usually chosen based on your personal constitution (known as *dosha* in Ayurvedic medicine).

Craniosacral Therapy

Another treatment that focuses on the Aries-ruled head is craniosacral therapy. The term *craniosacral* refers to the cranium (the head) and the sacrum (the bone in the lower back). This very gentle form of bodywork relieves tension and enhances the circulation of cerebrospinal fluid. A good portion of a craniosacral session involves the practitioner cradling and gently rocking your head, working to balance cranial rhythms and lightly adjusting the cranium bones. Reported benefits of this relaxing therapy include the reduction of chronic headaches and mental stress, and the relief of neck and back pain.

★ Craniosacral therapy is practiced by osteopaths, chiropractors, physical therapists, and massage therapists. As one of the more gentle treatments, it is a common form of bodywork used on children.

Moxibustion

Akin to acupuncture, moxibustion is a treatment widely used in traditional Asian medicine to address a wide range of health imbalances. Yet unlike acupuncture, moxibustion is noninvasive, using the power of Arien heat to induce healing. Practitioners either hold a stick of burning dried moxa (mugwort herb) above a target spot or place a heated kernel of it directly on the skin, oftentimes on top of a slice of Aries-ruled ginger. Moxibustion is said to stimulate the circulation of blood as well as the vital energy known as chi.

★ Practitioners can use moxibustion in combination with acupuncture. Warming an inserted needle with a moxa stick is said to further its ability to stimulate energy flow.

RELAXATION PRACTICES

Engaging in activities that give your fiery spirit a vehicle for expression can be very grounding and calming to an Arien.

Walking Meditation

If the idea of meditation intrigues you but you find the thought of sitting still for twenty minutes an unattractive prospect, walking meditation may be right up your alley. During this relaxation exercise, you focus your attention on your breath and/or a mantra while meandering in a predetermined path, whether around your neighborhood or your dining room table.

★ As in other forms of meditation, it's normal if thoughts come into your mind. Notice them and then let them pass, returning your attention to your breath or mantra. While some people find silence golden during this practice, others find it easier to concentrate while listening to a meditation CD.

Martial Arts

Participating in one of the many martial arts practices will help you get in touch with your inner warrior while providing a fun (and intense) workout. The martial arts are an effective way to get in shape, relieve stress, and gain the confidence that comes from knowing how to defend yourself. Since you can choose from a variety of traditions—including tae kwon do, aikido, kendo, and judo—you're sure to find one that suits your personal style.

★ Look online for studios (known as *dojos*) in your area. Many will allow you to observe classes before signing up so you can see whether the particular practice methods are of interest to you.

Fiery Crafts

As Ariens are blessed with creativity, and since the element of fire is associated with your sign, why not channel your artistic energy by crafting objects using the power of flame? Take a glassblowing class and transform molten glass into radiant objects of beauty. If making jewelry is of more interest, consider metalworking. As your sign is associated with iron, you could also try your hand at blacksmithing.

★ Art schools and community colleges are your best bets for learning these crafts. Survey courses will introduce you to a range of techniques so you can see which one is most appealing.

 **YOGA POSES**

Yoga can provide another form of exercise through which Ariens can channel their stockpiles of energy. There are many different styles of yoga to practice, allowing you to indulge your desire for variety.

Wide-Legged Forward Bend (*Prasarita Padottanasana*)

This forward bend allows you to experience having your head below your heart in a supported way. A good posture for headache relief, this pose brings blood to the head and brain and calms the nervous system.

★ Standing tall with your hands on your hips, walk your feet apart so they are about four feet from each other, keeping them parallel. Gently bend forward from the hips, keeping your back straight and placing your hands on the floor beneath your shoulders. Bend your elbows and allow your head to move toward the floor. If your head is close to the ground but can't reach it, place a folded blanket or yoga block underneath for support.

Warrior I Pose (*Virabhadrasana I*)

Warrior I Pose is perfect for the pioneering and champion-spirited Arien, reflecting the energy of the hero who conquers adversaries. This pose of strength and stability heats up the legs and moves the blood through the whole body.

★ Standing tall with your hands on your hips, walk your feet apart so they are about three feet from each other. Turn your right foot to the right 90 degrees and your left foot 30 degrees in the same direction. Then pivot your pelvis to the right, so that it is parallel with the front of your mat. Lift your arms straight up over your head without scrunching your shoulders, and then bend your right knee so it is in line with your right ankle. Hold for up to sixty seconds, and repeat on the other side.

Head-to-Knee Forward Bend (*Janu Sirsasana*)

This seated forward bend is calming to the brain and is said to relieve headaches and lower high blood pressure.

★ Sit on the floor on a folded blanket, with your legs straight in front of you. Bend your right knee and place the sole of your foot against your inner left thigh, resting your outer right leg on the floor with your shin at about a 90-degree angle to your left leg (if your right leg doesn't reach the floor, place a folded blanket underneath to support it). Turn your torso to face your left leg. Grab your left foot with both hands (or use a strap if that is too challenging). Push your left thigh into the floor, extend through your left foot, and then bend forward to bring your extended torso toward your thigh. Hold for sixty seconds, and repeat on the other side.

AROMATHERAPY

Aromatherapy can provide the Arien warrior with a fragrant way to defend well-being that doesn't require much of a time commitment.

Ginger (*Zingiber officinale*)

With its name derived from the Sanskrit word for *horn*, ginger essential oil is well suited for Rams and their wellness needs. It is an effective oil for muscle aches due to overexertion during exercise. And if you're prone to motion sickness, ginger essential oil may do the trick, as it is one of the best steadying remedies around. In addition, its warming fragrance inspires passion, and you can use it if you ever need to stoke your libidinal fire.

★ Add ginger and lemon juice to a bath for a pick-me-up when you feel under the weather. Use ginger-scented massage oil as a healing salve for sore muscles. Ginger oil can cause photosensitivity, so avoid using it if you're heading out into the sun.

Vetiver (*Vetiveria zizanioides*)

If you run yourself ragged and need a little rejuvenation, vetiver can help. It calms an overactive Arien mind, counters mental and physical exhaustion, and is used in Ayurvedic medicine for treating headaches. Its sweet and woody fragrance is said to dispel heat from both the body and the mind, which is one of the reasons for its calming effects and ability to temper irritability.

★ Carry a bottle of vetiver in your purse, inhaling its essence when you need a bit of extra calm. As the fragrance of vetiver mixes nicely with other oils and helps their scents last longer, experiment mixing it with your favorite natural perfumes.

Black Pepper (*Piper nigrum*)

Pungent, hot, and intense are three words that as readily describe an Arien as they do black pepper. This oil's warming properties increase circulation to the skin, help heal bruises, and relieve sore muscles. Its inspiring aroma also lifts the mood and energizes the body.

★ Instill the atmosphere with some "rise-and-shine" energy by using black pepper oil in a diffuser. Add a drop or two to body lotion, and apply to sore muscles or bruised areas. Always dilute this strong essence in an oil or cream before applying it to your skin.

NATURAL REMEDIES

Supplements, herbs, and homeopathics can be a first line of defense against many everyday health challenges.

Iron Supplements

Iron is a mineral that keeps the Aries-ruled blood oxygenated. If you suspect your diet isn't providing you with enough, consider taking some as a dietary supplement. While iron supplements come in a variety of forms, you might want to avoid ferrous sulfate as it can cause nausea and constipation in some people. Instead consider easy-to-assimilate chelated types, which aren't known for gastro-intestinal side effects. If you want iron in a nonpill form, look for a liquid iron supplement made from fruits, vegetables, and herbs.

★ Take your iron supplement with some orange juice, as vitamin C helps boost the mineral's absorption. While too little iron is problematic, so is too much; if you supplement with this nutrient, have your physician regularly monitor your iron levels.

Nettle (*Urtica dioica*)

Nettle is one of the main herbal remedies used for hay fever, a reaction to the pollen released by the flowers and trees that bloom during the Arien season of spring. Stumbling onto a patch of stinging nettle is hardly a healing experience, but with its poisonous bristles deactivated—by cooking, drying, or crushing—this herb's amazing health-promoting compounds are able to shine.

★ Nettle is available in capsule or liquid tincture form. You can also enjoy fresh nettle leaves, boiled or steamed in soups and other dishes.

Homeopathic Arnica

Homeopathic arnica is a very useful addition to an Arien's first-aid kit. Right after an injury occurs, especially a muscular strain or sprain, take arnica to reduce any associated pain and swelling. It's also great for soothing bruises and relieving muscle soreness caused by overexertion. And, if you're scheduled for dental work, arnica's anti-inflammatory properties may be just what the doctor ordered.

★ Mint and coffee can counteract the effectiveness of homeopathic remedies, so avoid them for several hours before and after taking arnica. In addition to arnica pills, this homeopathic remedy is also available as an ointment or gel for topical applications.

 # FLOWER ESSENCES

Vibrational elixirs that catalyze psycho-emotional healing, flower essences are made from flower blossoms, perfect for the Arien since your sign represents the birth and blooming inherent in springtime. All flower essences can be used similarly: mix a few drops in a glass of water, and drink several times a day; add some to a bath; or place in a water-filled mister bottle to enhance your environment.

Impatiens (*Impatiens glandulifera*)

Let's face it, as an Arien, patience isn't one of your strong suits. While you love the thrill of beginning new projects, you always itch to move on to the next experience. When your creative undertakings don't wrap up in an expeditious manner, your patience can run thin, potentially leading to bursts of anger that may cause you, and those around you, undue stress. As its name implies, Impatiens flower essence is a perfect remedy to subdue the hot-tempered Arien's proclivity for impatience.

Tiger Lily (*Lilium humboldtii*)

As an independent and pioneering Arien, you're a master at expressing your will in the pursuit of a goal. Yet sometimes others may perceive your assertiveness as bordering on aggressiveness, which may dampen their desire to provide you with support and cooperation. Given the Arien go-it-alone nature, this may not bother you as much as the next. Yet there are still times when collaborative service is more efficient (let alone more enjoyable) than solitary action. Helping one move from a tendency toward isolation to selectively opting for coalition is the realm of Tiger Lily flower essence.

Larkspur (*Delphinium nuttallianum*)

The take-charge attitude and zest for life of Ariens make them born leaders, a role to which you are naturally inclined but that doesn't come without its own set of challenges. Sometimes the responsibility of being at the helm can weigh you down. Other times it is difficult not to slip into feeling an imbalanced sense of self-importance when given a position of authority. When you find it more stressful than joyful to motivate others toward a collective goal, consider using the flower essence Larkspur. It can help an Arien's natural leadership instincts bloom.

taurus

SUN IN TAURUS ★ April 20–May 20

CHARACTERISTICS ★ Sensual / Grounded / Patient / Steadfast / Stubborn / Predictable / Creative / Self-indulgent / Practical / Kindhearted / Serene / Security oriented

SYMBOL ★ The *Bull*, an animal known for its strength, stamina, and grounded presence. Content on its own, it will become agitated if bothered by sudden movement. In mythological and cultural traditions, the Bull is a symbol of wealth, fertility, and stalwart power.

PLANETARY RULER ★ *Venus*, known for being the brightest planet in our solar system. Venus was the Roman goddess of beauty and love, who represented sexuality, pleasure, and fertility. Her counterpart in Greek mythology was Aphrodite. In astrology, Venus represents sensuality, harmony, and the force of attraction.

ELEMENT ★ *Earth*, characterized by the grounded energy of creativity, resistance, and practicality. It is fertile and passive, and it relates to the world on a sensual level.

QUALITY ★ *Fixed*, which represents the planning and building phase of the creative cycle. It reflects reliability, predictability, and a disciplined force that persists in creating structure.

Taureans have hardy constitutions and great physical resources. Like your astrological totem, the Bull, you are made of strong stock. Therefore, you are likely to be resistant to many illnesses to which others may be susceptible. However, as a fixed earth sign, when you do get sick, you go down for the count, and it takes awhile for you to fully recuperate, as Taureans need time to rebuild their momentum and regain their grounding.

As stress greatly affects your physical health, keep in mind that change represents some of the most taxing conditions for the security-oriented Bull. When you feel that your sense of stability is being threatened or find yourself worrying about pending life changes, it's important to build in extra time to relax and pamper yourself.

Taureans are known for having highly attuned senses. Therefore, massages, body wraps, moisturizing treatments, and other sensually pleasing wellness therapies are sure to appeal to the tactile Bull who likes being pampered. Those born under your sign are more than willing to expend time and resources to take care of themselves, especially if the experience allows them to indulge their senses.

As the gourmets of the zodiac, Taureans love food. Being so keenly aware of, and grounded in, your body, you're likely to be in tune with which foods will best meet your nutritional needs. However, your appreciation of food—and the pleasure it brings—may make it hard for you to curb your appetite. Maintaining an ideal weight is a challenge for a Taurean, especially later in life.

Not surprisingly, Bulls are famous for their bullheadedness, with a stubborn nature that makes it challenging to take advice from others, including health-care practitioners. Your routines are like a security blanket, and you hold on to them despite the toll they may take on your well-being. For your overall wellness, it's important to consider new health habits that may better serve your greater goals. Just think, once you get into the rhythm of these new ways, they'll bring you the comfort of having a ritual *and* the peace of mind that comes from knowing you are doing the best for your well-being.

 AREAS OF HEALTH FOCUS

Each zodiac sign is associated with certain parts of the body. These may be inherent areas of vulnerability, but when attended to, they can become areas of strength. The parts of the body associated with Taurus include the following:

★ The **throat**, which enables you to voice your truth

★ The **thyroid gland**, which regulates your metabolism and calcium levels

★ The **neck** and **cervical spine**, which allow you to hold your head high

★ The inner **ears** through which you experience sound and a sense of equilibrium

Your Taurean creativity, persistence, and practicality are some of the resources you can use when facing any health challenge.

Protect Your Throat

The cold and flu season is a rather quiet time for Taureans; after all, it's difficult to make much noise when you have a sore throat and laryngitis, common Taurean complaints. To maintain the health of the Taurus-ruled throat region throughout the year, adopt the habit of drinking plenty of water each day. Throat-soothing teas—many of which contain the herbs marshmallow root and slippery elm—with a touch of added honey make a delightful beverage. Also make sure your diet provides you with ample amounts of nutrients—notably immune-supportive vitamin C, zinc, and flavonoids—to help ward off infections.

Support Thyroid Health

Taurus rules the thyroid, the butterfly-shaped gland that produces hormones that regulate the body's metabolic rate and calcium levels. An overactive thyroid will result in your body burning energy too quickly while an underactive one can lead to a slowdown in metabolism, with ensuing weight gain. Thyroid imbalances often fly under the radar: they affect one in twenty people, although most don't know it. If thyroid hormone production is off-kilter, it can affect your mood balance, energy level, and menstruation cycle. If these symptoms ring a bell, it's worth discussing with your doctor, who can order a simple test to evaluate your thyroid hormone levels.

Prevent Pains in the Neck

Taurus also governs the neck, making this part of your body a sensitive one, likely to play host to stress and tension. Luckily, you can do some practical things to help reduce neck stiffness and pain. Maintaining good posture—keeping your neck in a neutral position—is key. If you work at a computer, this means adjusting your desk and chair height so that the top of your monitor is at eye level. Using a pillow with a shape that cradles your neck and supports its natural curve is also important. Doing gentle neck rolls and giving yourself frequent five-minute massages can help prevent neck cricks and discomfort.

Guard Ear Health

Taureans are all ears; you're a patient listener who sympathizes with others and their desire to communicate their values and needs. As your sign rules this part of the body, it's important to pay extra attention to your ears and protect your hearing. Ear infections or inflammation in this sensitive body part are often caused by allergies, sinusitis, or concomitant throat infections. Use earplugs when you're exposed to loud, potentially hearing-harmful sounds, whether from a concert or a neighbor's lawn mower. (Since a Taurean likes to always be prepared for the unexpected, keep a pack or two in your bag so they'll be handy when you need them.) For acute infections, try natural eardrops made from garlic, mullein, and St. John's wort.

 HEALTHY EATING TIPS

As an earth sign, Taureans clearly understand how food can nurture their physical health and as sensualists you also derive much pleasure from food. As you're likely to be fixed in your ways, if you identify an eating habit you'd like to change, be patient and courageous in your undertaking.

Love Food While Loving Your Health

When it comes to being the epicures of the zodiac, Taureans take the cake. You love food—shopping for it, preparing it, and, of course, eating it. Food nourishes your senses, the Taurean GPS that helps you navigate life. It also provides you with a feeling of being grounded, something that all earth signs crave. The obvious challenge for a Taurean food lover is preserving your culinary enjoyment while maintaining your waistline and health.

★ Today with the abundance of whole foods cookbooks and websites, learning to prepare great tasting food that's great for you has never been easier. To eat well and eat for wellness, shop at farmers' markets where you can find heirloom and exotic varieties of fruits, vegetables, whole grains, and other nutrient-rich fare that will delight the foodie in you.

Enjoy Homegrown Food

As the first earth sign, Taurus is very connected to the land. Tending a garden and growing your own food, therefore, is something you'd probably dig. Plus, as a sign that appreciates the value of money, a Taurean will also treasure gardening as an economical approach to enjoying delicious fresh vegetables and fruits.

★ Vegetable gardens let you experience the joy of nurturing the land and having it, in turn, nurture you through its bountiful harvest. If you are new to gardening, you can keep it simple by planting one or two types of easy-to-grow salad greens. If space permits, consider creating a mini home orchard by planting low-maintenance fruit trees. Taurean apartment dwellers can exercise their green thumbs by growing windowsill gardens of culinary herbs.

Incrementally Change Your Eating Habits

Taureans are creatures of habit. You derive great comfort from personal rituals, even if they are not the most supportive of your optimal well-being. For example, you may know that your afternoon triple latte isn't the best use of calories, but that doesn't make it any easier to forgo that three o'clock routine.

★ A great way to override your hesitation to change is just to dig your heels in and commit to it, knowing that in the end you'll be the better for it. Once you do so, use your stubborn and steadfast nature to your advantage to help you make the transition and stick to your new regimen. Pretty soon you'll get into the groove and the natural rhythms of your adopted healthful habit, comforted and supported by your new routine.

 ## HEALTH-SUPPORTING FOODS

Fruit and honey are both nutrient-rich ways to satisfy a Taurean sweet tooth. Very resourceful, the Bull may also appreciate using fresh garden herbs, since a little of each goes a long way to add flavor and health-promoting benefits to meals.

Fruit

Eating a variety of fruit can help Taureans bring their health goals to fruition. Fruit is a low-calorie way to curb sugar cravings, allowing you to stick to a diet while still indulging your desire for sweets. They are a source of quick, nutrient-rich energy that can put a spring in the step of the most grounded Bull.

★ For optimal health, consume at least two to three servings of fruit each day. While juice can play a role in a healthy diet, don't treat it as a substitute for whole fruit, since it contains very little, if any, fiber and has less beta-carotene and flavonoid phytonutrients.

Honey

Looking for an alternative to refined table sugar? Consider honey. Not only does honey add sweetness to foods and beverages but it's also a whole food that contains antioxidant and anticancer properties. In addition, honey mixed with warm water and a little lemon juice can offer much-needed relief from the sore throats to which Taureans are especially susceptible.

★ For greater nutritional benefits, including more antioxidant phytonutrients and cold-combating propolis, purchase raw honey rather than
the pasteurized variety (unless you're pregnant or nursing, in which
case raw honey is not recommended). Raw honey can be found in natural food stores and farmers' markets. Using local honey, produced
closest to where you live, is thought to ameliorate allergy symptoms.

Garden Herbs

Parsley, sage, rosemary, and thyme: More than just a good lyri-
cal refrain, this quartet of herbs can be one of the best additions
to a Taurean menu. They're an inexpensive way to add flavor to
your meals and, even when used in small amounts, add a wealth
of nutrients to your diet. In addition, they are easy to grow, something the practical and nature-loving Taurean will appreciate.

★ Garnish your health by including parsley in soups, stews, and salads.
Add sage to your tomato sauce the next time you make pasta. Rosemary makes a great seasoning for chicken dishes. Thyme is a flavorful
addition to scrambled eggs and omelets.

 # SPA AND WELLNESS THERAPIES

Spa and wellness therapies that delight your senses—especially
smell, touch, and hearing—and that use natural, food-based ingredients are very healing for a Taurean.

Aromatherapy Massage

An aromatherapy massage is perfect for a sensually oriented Taurean as it indulges two of your senses—touch and smell—at one
time. During this treatment, the practitioner prepares a custom-

blended massage oil from fragrant aromatherapy essences that meet your specific wellness needs. For example, clary sage and rose oils are used to elevate energy levels, while lavender and chamomile oils are good for relaxation.

★ Most practitioners use the Swedish style of massage during this treatment. If you'd prefer a different type of massage (for example, deep tissue or pregnancy), inquire about its availability. Also, if you have a penchant for certain fragrances, request they be used in your massage.

Food-Based Body Treatments

As you find food so nurturing, why not let it nourish your skin? Relax as you're slathered with coconut milk, avocado, or mangoes as part of a body-moisturizing regimen. Or enjoy an invigorating exfoliation treatment that uses pomegranate, rice bran, or cacao to help you shed dead skin. Not only do food-based spa treatments offer a bevy of beauty benefits, but they also provide a calorie-free sensual feast.

★ When considering food-based treatments, it's important to let the practitioner know about any allergies you may have. For example, if you're allergic to ragweed, you'll probably want to avoid treatments that feature bananas or melons, as you may also be sensitive to these ingredients. For simple at-home treatments, use avocado for a facial mask, coconut oil as a body moisturizer, and very finely ground almonds to exfoliate your skin.

Sonopuncture

Taureans experience the world through their senses, including hearing the sounds, and feeling the vibrations, all around them. Therefore, the healing technique of sonopuncture, which focuses on stimulating energy meridians through the use of rhythmic sound waves, is perfectly tuned to your health needs. Sonopuncture practitioners use special tuning forks, calibrated for different vibrations, which they gently apply to acupuncture points to bring about energetic harmony. Since this therapy is noninvasive and relaxing, it should ring true for the pleasure-loving Taurean.

★ Sonopuncture is also known as *tone acupuncture*. As the foundation of this healing art focuses on acupuncture points and energy meridians, acupuncturists are those you are most likely to find practicing sonopuncture.

 RELAXATION PRACTICES

Since Taureans need to feel grounded and secure to be at ease, activities that connect you with the Earth can be a very fruitful way to relax.

Pottery

Working with clay is a great way for a Taurean to relax. It provides you with an opportunity to interact directly with an earth element, creating objects that have both beauty and function. Clay's malleability allows you to build and rebuild your pottery piece. From this art form, the fixed-nature Taurean can directly experience the power of change as a valuable part of creativity instead of as a process to fear.

★ The two main methods of creating pottery are wheel throwing and hand building. In wheel throwing, you sit at a potter's wheel and, aided by its spinning motion, shape the clay. Hand building offers a slower process that allows for greater control over the form you construct.

Communing with Nature

As an earth sign, being among the flora and fauna is key to a Taurean developing a sense of inner peace. Whether you spend the day hiking in the hills or just twenty minutes strolling in a city park, getting out into nature will help you connect with the Earth's natural rhythms, which that are so nourishing for your soul.

★ In addition to walking, you can do many everyday things to keep connected to nature. Watch the birds take flight and listen to their magical songs. Plant your bare feet in the soil. Get grounded by digging the dirt in your vegetable garden or flowerbed.

Music

As Taureans are acutely attuned to the aural realms, playing or listening to music can be an incredibly relaxing pastime. Music stimulates the throat and ears (in addition to the soul), parts of the body ruled by your sign. If you are caught in a labyrinth of looping thoughts, listening to music can help you find your way out.

★ Try your hand at playing an instrument, whether you strum a guitar or beat on some bongos. Or sing, even if it's just when you're in the shower, to help you connect with your voice. Music is inspiring and experiencing sounds that you have created is empowering.

 **YOGA POSES**

Yoga can be a great way for a Taurean to gain more flexibility. Poses that focus on the neck, cervical spine, and thyroid gland can be particularly beneficial.

Cow Pose (*Bitilasana*)

Named after your astrological totem, Cow Pose is perfect for the slow and steady rhythm of a Taurean. A great posture for coordinating movement with breathing, Cow Pose enhances the flexibility of the neck and warms up the spine.

★ Place your hands and knees on the floor in the tabletop position (your knees should align directly below your hips, with your elbows and wrists below your shoulders). Your neck should be in a neutral position with your eyes gazing toward the floor. While inhaling, lift your chest and sit bones toward the ceiling while dropping your belly to create a gentle arch in your back. Lift your head and look straight in front of you. Hold for several seconds. Exhale, draw your belly in, and move your spine back to the tabletop position for several seconds. Repeat the sequence eight to twelve times.

Bridge Pose (*Setu Bandha Sarvangasana*)

When your grounded nature needs an energizing lift, try Bridge Pose. This all-over workout awakens the senses and is especially beneficial for neck and thyroid health.

★ Lie flat on your back with your knees bent and your feet hip distance apart. (For extra neck support, place a folded blanket underneath your shoulders.) To ensure proper foot placement, extend your arms along the ground, and place your heels in the spot where they touch your fingertips. With your feet flat on the floor, lift your hips. With your arms straight, clasp your hands behind your back. Stay in the pose for up to sixty seconds. When finished, gently roll down vertebra by vertebra on an exhalation.

Staff Pose (*Dandasana*)

This pose, named for the straight rodlike positioning of your spine, is the foundation for many other seated postures. While it seems basic, it has numerous benefits including energizing your whole body and stretching your neck muscles.

★ Sit on the floor with your legs extended straight in front of you. Adjust your buttocks so your sit bones are on the floor (if your back isn't straight, consider sitting on a folded blanket). Without locking your knees, activate your legs by pushing your thighs into the floor and extending out through your flexed feet. Move your shoulder blades down your back, and rest your hands on the floor beside you. Lengthen your spine so it is perpendicular to the floor, and then gently bring your chin toward your chest. Stay in the pose for at least one minute.

 AROMATHERAPY

Attuned to their senses, through which they navigate the world, Taureans can derive great pleasure from beautiful fragrances.

Vanilla (*Vanilla planifolia*)

The essential oil of vanilla smells good enough to eat. Deliciously grounding and relaxing, vanilla is well known for its aphrodisiac properties, something that sensual Taureans will appreciate. Mexican legend tells a tale of how vanilla came to be: a goddess, unable to wed the mortal she loved, transformed herself into a vanilla plant as a way to provide him with constant delight.

★ Vanilla makes a lovely perfume either alone or mixed with other fragrances. Look for high quality vanilla oil because the less expensive ones may be synthetically derived. If you can't find a pure essence, make your own by steeping chopped vanilla pods in jojoba oil.

Palmarosa (*Cymbopogon martini*)

Tall grass plants, like the one from which palmarosa essential oil is distilled, sway fluidly in the wind without losing their structural integrity. Palmarosa inspires this same feeling of secure movement in those who wear it, making it a perfect fragrance for the steadfast Taurean. Endowed with a sweet citrus-rose scent, palmarosa is also used in many skin-care products for its antiseptic and moisture-balancing properties.

★ When using palmarosa as a perfume, dab some behind your Taurus-ruled ears. Put several drops in a misting bottle filled with water to make a refreshing skin toner, or add some to your moisturizer. When your feet get tired, soak them in a palmarosa-infused footbath.

Thyme (*Thymus vulgaris*)

Throughout history, thyme has been heralded as an herb that promotes courage. Therefore, using thyme essential oil is good for a Taurean, whose slow-moving nature can sometimes use a little prod to push through barriers. Thyme can also be used as an antimicrobial agent, digestive aid, and scalp tonic.

★ To benefit from its antimicrobial and mood-elevating properties, use thyme oil in a diffuser. Add a few drops to your shampoo bottle to enjoy its scalp-nourishing attributes. Thyme oil is very strong and may cause reactions if used directly on the skin; dilute it in oil, lotion, or liquid soap before using.

NATURAL REMEDIES

Appreciative of the bounty that nature yields, Taureans understand the healing benefits that herbs, dietary supplements, and other natural remedies can provide.

Marshmallow (*Althea officinalis*)

For those pesky sore throats, try some marshmallow: the root from the *Althea officinalis* plant, not, unfortunately, the confection of the same name that lends its sweet gooeyness to campfire s'mores. Long used in traditional medicine to treat sore throats and coughs, marshmallow root was the main ingredient in a popular brand of nineteenth-century children's lozenges.

★ This throat-soothing herb is available in dried form or as a liquid tincture, either of which you can use to make a restorative tea. You can also find marshmallow as an ingredient in therapeutic tea blends that contain the herb slippery elm.

Chlorophyll-Containing Supplements

Chlorophyll allows plants to transform light into energy. It also gives plants their green color. If your diet doesn't contain a lot of leafy green vegetables, you may want to consider adding a chlorophyll-rich food supplement—such as wheat grass, barley grass, or blue-green algae—to your wellness repertoire. In addition to health-promoting chlorophyll, these supplements contain a range of other energy-producing nutrients.

★ Green food supplements are available as tablets or powders, the latter being a great addition to smoothies. Chlorophyll supplements can also be found in liquid form, which you can use to help combat bad breath, should that be a concern.

Homeopathic Belladonna

Reflective of an association with Venus, your planetary ruler, *belladonna* means "beautiful woman" in Italian. Belladonna is a homeopathic remedy effective for many Taurean complaints including sore throats, stiff necks, and earaches. It's particularly beneficial for those with stress caused by sudden movement and those sensitive to cold: characteristics of many Taureans.

★ Homeopathic remedies are extremely diluted forms of the natural substance from which they are made. This is the reason that homeopathic belladonna is safe, but consuming the plant itself isn't. Mint and coffee can counteract the effectiveness of homeopathic remedies, so avoid them for several hours before and after taking belladonna.

FLOWER ESSENCES

Once you experience the healing results of flower essences and how they can help create balance on a psycho-emotional level, you will likely adopt these holistic remedies as a new wellness habit. All flower essences can be used similarly: mix a few drops in a glass of water, and drink several times a day; add some to a bath; or place in a water-filled mister bottle to enhance your environment.

Chestnut Bud (*Aesculus hippocastanum*)

For a Taurean, the "been there, done that" idiom comes with a twist. For you, it's "been there, done that, now I'll do that again." More comfortable with the known than the unknown, you often repeat an action or stay with a habit even if it hasn't paid off in the past. The flower essence Chestnut Bud is perfect for times when you want a little help breaking free from routines that provide you not with growth but only the comfort of familiarity.

Iris (*Iris douglasiana*)

Taureans make great artists. You have a visceral knowingness for what pleases the senses and the aptitude to create beauty from natural materials. Like many artists, you're probably intermittently plagued by self-doubt and what at times feels like an insurmountable barrier between yourself and your inner creativity. When you're looking for the energy of a muse, try Iris flower essence. It can help reopen those channels of inspiration.

Hound's Tongue (*Cynoglossum grande*)

Taureans are straight shooters who often live by the adage "What you see is what you get." As a practical and materially oriented sign, you take things at face value. Yet the complexities of life can sometimes call for going below the surface to examine the subtleties of a situation and the often hidden value that things inherently contain. When you need a little assistance delving deeper, try Hound's Tongue flower essence.

gemini

SUN IN GEMINI ★ May 21–June 21

CHARACTERISTICS ★ Curious / Dual natured / Talkative / Adaptable / Quick-witted / Youthful / Mercurial / Fickle / Cunning / Spontaneous / Observant / Informative

SYMBOL ★ The *Twins*, biological siblings who share a commonality while also expressing unique individuality. In mythological and cultural traditions, Twins are a symbol of the dualistic, yin and yang aspects that constitute the essence of the whole.

PLANETARY RULER ★ *Mercury*, which has the fastest orbit around the Sun. Mercury was the Roman god of commerce, known for his role as the messenger of the gods. His counterpart in Greek mythology was Hermes. In astrology, Mercury represents communication, intellect, language, and bridge building.

ELEMENT ★ *Air*, characterized by the agile energy of thoughts, observation, and logic. It is social, intellectual, changeable, and relationship oriented.

QUALITY ★ *Mutable*, which represents the adjustment and finessing stage of the creative cycle. It reflects flexibility, tolerance, and an adaptive and transformative free-flowing force.

A Gemini loves to solve problems of all kinds, and those involving your health are no exception. With your keen curiosity and need-to-know nature, you'll wade through books, websites, and medical journals—and pick the brain of anyone in the know—in your quest to find the best treatment plan to cure your ailment or enhance your well-being. The road to wellness is an intellectual challenge that fascinates a Gemini. The process of finding the answer is as interesting to you as the answer itself.

While those born under the sign of the Twins like thinking about health solutions, committing to the action steps required can sometimes pose a challenge. One key to success is finding a wellness prescription that gives you a flexible structure while fulfilling your need for variety. For example, block off a specific window of time each day for exercising; then, depending on your mood, choose whether to walk, swim, practice yoga, or another of your favorite activities.

Also, when you try to solve a health conundrum, why limit yourself to one natural remedy or body-mind therapy? A well-researched assortment of self-care approaches will keep you from getting bored—the bane of a Gemini's existence—and will appeal to the various, and sometimes competing, aspects of your personality. (While the symbolic depiction of your astrological sign is a set of Twins, with the multitude of perspectives they hold, Geminis may sometimes feel more like octuplets.) One of the most beneficial yet challenging goals for Geminis is to synthesize all parts of their multifaceted being. Therefore, an approach to health that honors your diversified preferences will not only prove interesting to you but healing as well.

Since Geminis are communicators par excellence, it's very important for you to seek out and work with health-care practitioners who match you on this level. Seek out those who listen well: not only are the Twins adept at describing their state of health in detail, but they also find the act of being listened to instrumental to feeling their very best. The best health-care guide for a Gemini is someone who provides you with plenty of information and resources. After all, knowledge is power—and the source of your personal empowerment.

 ## AREAS OF HEALTH FOCUS

Each zodiac sign is associated with certain parts of the body. These may be inherent areas of vulnerability, but when attended to, they can become areas of strength. The parts of the body associated with Gemini include the following:

★ The **lungs**, which provide your blood with the vital oxygen it needs to energize your body and mind

★ The **nervous system**, the inner switchboard that processes information from your internal and external environments

★ The **arms**, one of the twin parts of the body, from the shoulders all the way down to the fingers

Your Gemini communication skills, adaptable nature, and curious mind are some of the resources you can use when facing any health challenge.

Safeguard Respiratory Health

As Gemini governs the lungs, you should take extra precautions to support respiratory health. Make sure to get an abundance of the "ACE" antioxidants (vitamins A, C, and E) in your diet, especially if you do a lot of cardiovascular exercise since it increases free radical activity in the lungs. If you have asthma or frequent respiratory colds, limit your intake of dairy products and food additives (such as the yellow dye #5 found in candy, a favorite Gemini treat) since these can exacerbate bronchial symptoms. Also pay attention to your breathing—something a busy Gemini can forget to do—making sure it's deep and rhythmic, because shallow breathing leads to reduced energy and a foggy mind.

Relieve Stress and Tension

Geminis love to gather data; your restless, quicksilver mind seeks every possible fact and figure in your quest for knowledge. While you feel drawn to this type of mental stimulation, you can also suffer from information overload, resulting in undue stress on your nervous system. This stress often manifests in muscular tension—notably in your shoulders—as well as a state of low-level anxiety. It's especially important for Geminis to tune out every now and then to recharge their batteries and replenish their health. Take periodic vacations from your cell phone, computer, and television, and schedule a little quiet time each day where you can tune out the world and tune into yourself.

Protect Your Arms

Geminis are masters of text messaging, remote controlling, mouse clicking, and gesticulating, all means by which you access and share information. What these activities also have in common is that they engage the arms in habitual motions that can tax muscles, tendons, and nerves, leading to repetitive stress injury. As you're unlikely to stop using electronic gadgets (or talking with your hands), safeguard your health by enhancing the ergonomics of your work space. Invest in a mouse or trackball that cradles your hand, a functionally designed keyboard that allows for more natural wrist positioning, and a high quality chair on which you can adjust the height and armrest position.

Watch Out for Accidents

As a Gemini, you're likely to be adept at multitasking. While performing many activities at once suits your restless and active spirit, it's not necessarily the best recipe for safety (especially if it's an activity that involves moving objects, such as talking on the phone while driving). Additionally, you may also run into problems—and three-dimensional objects—when you focus so intently on the inner landscape of your mind rather than the outer landscape of your environment. To mitigate your accident-prone nature, practice mindfulness, the art of being present in mind *and* body.

HEALTHY EATING TIPS

For a Gemini, the trick to eating a healthful diet is to make it interesting, enjoying an array of different whole foods that offer your mind and senses a range of experiences.

Eat Regularly

Geminis dislike routine, and the idea of regularly scheduled meals is no exception. When mealtime rolls around, you're likely to postpone it for something of more interest at that moment. The next thing you know, your blood sugar takes a nosedive and you grab anything, and everything, in sight with little regard to its healthfulness.

★ If you hate being pinned down to an exact mealtime, give yourself a more flexible two-hour window in which to enjoy your repast. If three squares a day doesn't work for you, consider five to six time-saving mini-meals. Having a consistent eating schedule is a good move when it comes to your physical health since it improves digestive function and better regulates appetite.

Slow Down

When Geminis do get around to eating, they often rush through it, regarding it as an unwanted distraction from their work project, social engagement, or sudoku puzzle. If you eat too fast, it can make your nerves jumpy, let alone lead to less-than-optimal absorption of nutrients. Eating slowly is not only a great mindfulness practice but can also help promote better nourishment.

★ Make your meals more interesting by combining foods that feature an assortment of colors, tastes, and textures. This more varied fare may help you slow down so you can really savor and enjoy your meal. You can also put your Gemini scribe into action, using it to enhance your meal-time mindfulness; keeping a journal with you at meals and writing up your impressions of your culinary experiences is a great way to enhance your awareness.

Stock the Basics

It's easy to identify a Gemini's kitchen. It's the one chock-full of condiments—a slew of salsas, an assortment of olive oils, a bounty of jams and jellies—and little else. Even if your cornucopia of condiments rivals that of the best gourmet store, without some pantry basics, it's difficult to make a satisfying and nourishing meal.

★ In addition to condiments, stock your kitchen with some nutrient-rich foundation foods to ensure that you always have the makings of a healthy and easy-to-prepare meal. Some of the basics include frozen vegetables, canned beans, brown rice, pasta, nuts, onions, and garlic.

 HEALTH-SUPPORTING FOODS

The Twins need variety in their diet so they don't get bored of eating healthfully. Luckily, some of the best Gemini foods—orange-colored fruits and vegetables, dairy-free milk alternatives, and oats—can be prepared and enjoyed in a range of different ways.

Orange Fruits and Vegetables

Beta-cryptoxanthin, an up-and-coming nutritional star, is a cousin of beta-carotene that offers great support for the health of the Gemini-ruled lungs. It's a powerful antioxidant that can be converted in the body to vitamin A and is thought to lower the risk of developing lung cancer.

★ While beta-cryptoxanthin may be hard to pronounce, you can easily identify foods rich in this phytonutrient: just look for deeply orange-colored fruits and vegetables. Carrots, butternut squash, pumpkins, papaya, sweet potatoes, and tangerines are among your best bets if you would like to enjoy this carotenoid's benefits.

Dairy-Free Milk Alternatives

While cow's milk and other dairy foods may be rich in calcium and other nutrients, many people are allergic to them. Asthma and other respiratory complaints are often linked to dairy allergies. If you're prone to these Gemini-related conditions, you may want to limit your intake of dairy products (or avoid them completely for a while) to see if your health improves.

★ If you're looking for dairy-free calcium contributors, try collard greens, kale, and spinach. You can find plenty of milk alternatives in the marketplace, including those made from soy beans, hemp seeds, and the Gemini favorite, oats. Some people with cow's milk allergies can tolerate goat's milk and products made from it.

Oats

Enjoying a bowl of oats—served hot as oatmeal or cold as muesli—is a great way for a Gemini to start the day. Not only do oats have cholesterol-lowering benefits, but they also help to soothe frayed nerves. Additionally, a breakfast containing oats can contribute to enhanced cognitive performance and sustained energy throughout the day.

★ Instead of instant oatmeal opt for rolled oats, which only take a few minutes to make but are much more nutritious. Add variety to your morning meal by alternating how you prepare the oats: try a sweet version topped with fruit and honey or a savory one mixed with spices and steamed vegetables. Oat milk, available in natural food stores, is a delicious dairy-free beverage to use in smoothies or hot chocolate or to drink straight from the glass.

SPA AND WELLNESS THERAPIES

Many spa and wellness therapies allow Geminis, so often in their mind, the ability to feel more grounded in their bodies while others can help them probe the mines of their mind even further to gain valuable insights.

Chair Massage

A wellness therapy that requires a minimal time commitment, chair massage is tailor-made for a Gemini. It usually lasts for only fifteen minutes, so you can enjoy one without taking too much time away from the many other items on your "to do" list. During this treatment, you rest fully clothed in a padded chair that allows you to relax your upper body. In addition to massaging your back and neck, the practitioner will work out the kinks and stress residing in your Gemini-ruled shoulders and arms.

★ Look for chair-massage kiosks in malls and airports. Many bodywork practitioners have their own massage chairs and do on-site work-place visits as well.

Manicures

Geminis' hands are their ambassadors to the world. They help you write, collect information, and meet and greet the many people with whom you interact. Plus, as the zodiac's premier gesticulators, Geminis rely on their hands to help them communicate and express their thoughts. So put your best hand forward by treating yourself to regular manicures.

★ Manicures aren't always expensive or time-consuming. Many salons offer express sessions that can give your hands a tune-up in a matter of minutes. Since salons range in how thoroughly they sanitize their tools, bring your own for optimal hygiene.

Talk Therapy

Gemini's planetary ruler, Mercury, is named after the winged-foot messenger god of Roman cosmology who easily crossed between the earth and the underworld during his appointed rounds. Geminis are adept at this Mercurial skill of traversing boundaries, which can be used to create a dialogue between the different levels of your mind. This gift, combined with your natural loquaciousness, makes talk therapy a beneficial healing approach for a Gemini.

★ Choose from numerous forms of talk therapy, including cognitive, behavioral, psychodynamic, and others. Take a little time to investigate the field and research local therapists to find the approach that is most appealing to you.

RELAXATION PRACTICES

Reflecting the opposing yet complementary Twins that symbolize your sign, both stimulating and centering your mind can be relaxing to a Gemini.

Games and Puzzles

While it may sound paradoxical, things that exhilerate Geminis' minds also relax them. Therefore, participating in games and doing puzzles are great activities if you want to unwind. Plus a night of games can be a fun activity for a social get-together, something the Twins cherish.

★ Jigsaw puzzles not only exercise your spatial capabilities, but they also offer built-in flexibility as you can finish the puzzle on your own timetable—a bonus for the busy Gemini. When you can't get friends and family together to play a group game such as Scrabble or Monopoly, don't despair; working a sudoku or crossword puzzle, or playing an old-fashioned game of solitaire, can be a very meditative experience.

Pranayama

Pranayama is the name used to describe various breathing exercises practiced in the yogic tradition. Doing *pranayama* helps expand concentration while calming the mind and is often done before meditation. It can also increase your awareness of your respiratory patterns, helping you catch any tendency you may have toward shallow breathing.

★ If you want to learn a few *pranayama* exercises, yoga classes are a great resource as they usually include some breathwork practice. Plus, while you do asanas (poses), most yoga teachers will invariably remind you to concentrate on your breath.

Journaling

Keeping a journal is a very helpful exercise for inventorying your thoughts and feelings. Whether it be stories, poems, or just random mind chatter, getting the words and ideas out of your head and onto the page—or the computer screen—can be a centering exercise for a Gemini. If you're so inclined, you could share your journal with others by offering it online as a blog.

★ Instead of using a basic spiral-bound notebook, find a colorful and artistically designed journal in which to keep your thoughts. To more clearly access your subconscious, try nondominant hand writing: righties use their left hand, and lefties use their right. While your writing may look like kindergarten scrawl, you'll be amazed at how it can quiet your mind and draw out some under-the-surface memories.

The mindfulness exercise practice of yoga can help enhance a Gemini's innate sense of flexibility, giving you an opportunity to move your body and feel centered in it.

Cobra Pose (*Bhujangasana*)

This mini-backbend is a great pose for reversing the effects of the slouching shoulders and compressed chest that can come from hours engaged in writing, surfing the Internet, catching up with friends online, or other activities that Geminis favor.

★ Lie facedown on your mat with the tops of your feet touching the floor. Place your hands on the ground next to your chest while keeping your elbows close to your body. On an inhalation, press your feet, legs, and pubic bone into the floor (where they should remain). Simultaneously, press through your palms, lifting your chest in a slight backward arc. Roll your shoulders back and down, and lift through your sternum (which will help you avoid compressing your lower back). Stay in the pose for up to thirty seconds. When ready to leave the pose, exhale, and come down slowly.

Dolphin Pose

Like a Gemini, dolphins are considered to be extremely intelligent. If you seek a posture that will help you stretch and strengthen your shoulders, arms, and wrists, Dolphin Pose is a smart choice.

★ Place your hands and knees on the floor in the tabletop position (your knees should align directly below your hips, with your elbows and wrists below your shoulders). Drop your elbows to the floor underneath your shoulders. Keeping your elbows in place, interlace your fingers together. Tuck your toes under, and send your hips toward the sky while pressing your forearms and wrists into the ground. The crown of your head should be facing the mat and contained within the triangle-shaped space created by your arms. Your knees can be straight or slightly bent, whichever allows your pelvis to lift away from your shoulders. Stay in the pose for up to sixty seconds.

Extended Side Angle Pose (*Utthita Parsvakonasana*)

Extended Side Angle Pose stretches and strengthens many parts of your body, including the shoulders, arms, and wrists. It's challenging to perform, let alone master, which is an extra perk for puzzle-solving Geminis.

★ Standing tall with your arms outstretched to each side and your palms facing up, walk your feet apart so they are about four feet from each other. Rotate your right foot 90 degrees toward the right and your left foot 45 degrees in the same direction. Bend your right knee so that your calf is perpendicular to the floor and your knee is over your ankle. Tilt your torso and pelvis to the right, and place your right forearm on your right thigh. Stretch your left arm over your ear and toward the right side so that you feel a lengthening through your left torso while trying to keep your right torso lengthened as well. Stay in the pose for up to sixty seconds, and then repeat on the other side.

AROMATHERAPY

That the aromas of essential oils are not only pleasing but can also have profound effects on health may be an enchanting idea to the mind of a Gemini.

Rosemary (*Rosmarinus officinalis*)

Since antiquity, when ancient Greek scholars wore rosemary wreaths to aid their studying, this herb has been esteemed for its ability to inspire concentration and fortify memory. Its rosmarinic acid component helps to calm the nerves, making it a relaxing tonic for a Gemini.

★ To benefit from a concentration-enhancing halo, mix a few drops of rosemary essential oil into your hair conditioner. Keep a bottle of rosemary on your desk, inhaling it any time you want to release stress and enhance your focus. Grow a rosemary plant on a sunny windowsill, and enjoy its aroma in your tea or lemonade.

Lavender (*Lavandula angustifolia*)

Like the Twins, Mercury-ruled lavender seems to have two different sides, both of which reflect the very useful properties of this popular essential oil. It has an attractive quality that comes from its sweetly floral and relaxing scent, making it a favored perfume. It also has an unattractive quality—to bugs, that is—making it a powerful antimicrobial agent and insect repellent.

★ Lavender is a lovely scent to wear; add some to your body lotion, or dab a few drops on your neck or wrist. Fill a small cloth bag with dried lavender buds, and use it as a drawer sachet to fragrance your clothes and keep pesky moths away from your prized sweaters.

Eucalyptus (*Eucalyptus globules*)

Eucalyptus essential oil makes a great addition to a Gemini first-aid kit. It is well known for its respiratory health properties: not only is it an effective expectorant, but research suggests that it has potent antimicrobial action against viruses and bacteria that cause bronchial infections. This fresh smelling oil can also help relieve muscle aches and pains.

★ Fill a basin with hot water, and add a few drops of eucalyptus oil for an inhalation treatment to relieve congested lungs and nasal passages. Mix some eucalyptus with coconut oil for an invigorating chest-rub ointment to help with respiratory ailments.

NATURAL REMEDIES

Geminis may find it fascinating to learn about all the different natural remedies they can use to customize their self-care regimen.

Bacopa (*Bacopa monniera*)

A Gemini loves to discover new things, and if it's something like the herb bacopa, which helps enhance your memory and concentration, all the better. While recent studies have shown its promising cognitive-enhancing effects, appreciation for bacopa's benefits is anything but new. This herb has been used for more than three thousand years in Ayurvedic medicine, where it is classified as a *medhya rasayana* (mind rejuvenator).

★ You can find bacopa in pure herb form or standardized to levels of bacosides A and B, two of its active compounds. In addition to using it as a supplement, in Ayurvedic practice, bacopa extract is mixed with massage oil and rubbed into the scalp as a stress-relieving treatment.

B-Complex Vitamins

B vitamins have a range of functions, including supporting energy production and maintaining the health of the nervous system. If your diet is not replete with whole grains, leafy greens, and legumes, you may want to consider taking a B-complex supplement, or at least be certain that your multivitamin provides adequate amounts of these nutrients. Some medications—including oral contraceptives and estrogens—deplete the body's store of B vitamins, making it even more important to ensure you get enough.

★ Take B vitamins with food to avoid stomach upset. As with all supplements, let your doctor know if you're considering a B complex so you can discover any interactions it may have with medications you may currently take.

Kali Mur Cell Salt

Kali mur is the name of the homeopathic cell salt made from potassium chloride, a mineral found in muscle, nerve, and brain cells. Associated with Gemini, this cell salt is involved in the expression and dispersion of energy. When anxiety and nervousness manifest and cloud mental clarity, kali mur is often suggested as a good remedy.

★ Cell salts like kali mur are available in health food stores and natural pharmacies. Mint and coffee can counteract the effectiveness of homeopathic remedies, so avoid them for several hours before and after taking kali mur.

 FLOWER ESSENCES

If you want to learn more about ways to balance your emotions and transform psychological challenges into strengths, flower essences are a great thing to investigate. All flower essences can be used similarly: mix a few drops in a glass of water, and drink several times a day; add some to a bath; or place in a water-filled mister bottle to enhance your environment.

White Chestnut (*Aesculus hippocastanum*)

A Gemini's mind usually spins with ideas. While numerous thoughts circulate through for your analysis and reflection, sometimes a particular one may get stuck—repeating itself again and again—in what seems like a perpetual mental merry-go-round. If you need help calming mind chatter and breaking the reins of looping thoughts, try White Chestnut flower essence.

Cosmos (*Cosmos bipinnatus*)

Geminis are lifelong curators of facts and figures. While your mind's gallery contains a vast collection of information, synthesizing the pieces into a whole can be a challenging pursuit, even for the intellectually oriented Twins. Cosmos flower essence helps to focus the mind and create a clear channel between thoughts and the spoken words used to express them. As such, it can be a great aid for public speaking.

Cerato (*Ceratostigma willmottiana*)

A Gemini's love of information often translates into seeking insights from other people—usually lots of other people. Yet if you rely on the advice of others too frequently, especially as a substitute for trusting your own inner voice, it can lead to confusion. Or worse, it can result in your acting in ways counter to your true nature. When you need a little boost of confidence in your own decision-making abilities, Cerato flower essence is definitely a good choice.

cancer

SUN IN CANCER ★ June 22–July 22

CHARACTERISTICS ★ Nurturing / Sensitive / Hospitable / Sympathetic / Indirect / Defensive / Nostalgic / Protective / Moody / Traditional / Unpredictable / Sentimental

SYMBOL ★ The *Crab*, a sea- and land-dwelling animal known for its hard shell that protects a soft interior and claws that defend and gather food. In mythological and cultural traditions, the Crab is a symbol of service, loyalty, bravery, and a nondirect approach to confrontation.

PLANETARY RULER ★ The *Moon*, a satellite of the Earth known for its cycles as well as reflecting the Sun's light. Selene was the Greek goddess of the Moon while the Roman goddess was known as Luna. In astrology, the Moon represents feelings, unconscious patterns, nurturance, and the mother.

ELEMENT ★ *Water*, characterized by the fluid energy of emotion, reflection, and nonlinear understanding. It is sensitive, personal, and responsive.

QUALITY ★ *Cardinal*, which represents the initiation of the creative cycle. It reflects ambition, enterprise, speed, and a self-starting force that propels energy into the world.

PERSONAL HEALTH PROFILE

Despite the Crab's defensive shell, within you resides a very sensitive soul whose physical health is highly influenced by an expansive reservoir of feelings. On occasion, a Cancerian may become captivated by a sense of moodiness that seems to come from nowhere, while in reality it springs from the deep sentimental undercurrents that live within. Accepting and expressing these emotions, rather than fearing and internalizing them, can do wonders for Cancerian health.

Those born under the sign of the Crab are very intuitive, often aware of—and able to remedy—symptoms of *dis*-ease before they transform into more serious illnesses. You're also especially attuned to the cycles of the Moon, your planetary ruler. This lunar alignment makes Cancerians cyclical creatures, whose moods, energy levels, and even water retention (and therefore, weight) wax and wane throughout the month. Knowing this about yourself is important in planning your health-care strategies. This wisdom can also prove calming to the Cancerian spirit by helping you realize that it is often periodicity that guides your feelings and physical health rather than unpredictability.

The Moon is the astrological symbol for the mother and, as such, represents feminine energy expressed through instinctive maternal sentiments. Cancerians, in accordance with their planetary ruler, possess great nurturing qualities. Not only do you like to care for others, you also like to be cared for; having another comfort you, even in the smallest of ways, can do wonders for your well-being. The trick to optimal health, though, is to refine your self-care abilities so you needn't be overly dependent on others.

With a strong reverence for all that came before, Crabs are often very traditional creatures. Since your temperament is more aligned with things that are tried and true, you're more likely to try one of the latest wellness trends if it's well rooted in the past. For example, folk remedies—including those handed down through the generations of your own family—appeal to this nostalgic orientation.

Your allegiance to time-honored traditions is bolstered by an inclination toward preventative medicine. The safety-seeking Crab is motivated to action by preservation and the reduction of perceived threats, illness included. Going to the doctor for routine visits is comforting to a Cancerian, especially if your health-care practitioner is a nurturing and kind soul.

 ## AREAS OF HEALTH FOCUS

Each zodiac sign is associated with certain parts of the body. These may be inherent areas of vulnerability, but when attended to, they can become areas of strength. The parts of the body associated with Cancer include the following:

★ The body's containers, such as the **stomach** and **sinuses**

★ The **esophagus**, the passageway through which food enters the stomach

★ The **breasts** and **womb**, symbols of femininity and nurturance

★ **Saliva**, **digestive juices**, and other **body fluids**

Your Cancerian caretaking nature, strong sense of intuition, and desire for self-protection are some of the resources you can use when facing any health challenge.

Trust Your Gut

In medical astrology, the stomach and esophagus are ruled by Cancer, making them two of the Crab's more vulnerable body spots. Reducing caffeine, watching out for food allergies, and eating slowly can help reduce heartburn as can natural remedies such as bromelain and slippery elm. While excess stomach acid can cause challenges, so can insufficient amounts. Often caused by the routine use of antacids, low stomach acid (hypochlorhydria) can lead to indigestion as well as malabsorption of protein, vitamin B12, and other nutrients. Bitter herbs such as gentian and celandine may be helpful for stimulating gastric acid production. Additionally, a Cancerian's stomach may often be tied in knots, especially if you tend to internalize your feelings rather than express them. Making time each day to relax can help pacify butterflies and calm a nervous stomach.

Soothe Your Sinuses

Sensitive to their environment, Cancerians are often allergy sufferers. And with your sign ruling the sinuses, allergies—as well as infections—in this part of the body may be common fare. The traditional route to quelling sinus infections includes antibiotics and decongestants. A preventative approach includes supplements such as n-acetyl-cysteine and vitamin C. The Ayurvedic practice of *jala neti*, nasal irrigation using a neti pot, can also be helpful for relieving sinus congestion. Additionally, watch out for food allergies; while Cancerians may gravitate toward milk and other dairy products because of their soothing texture, these foods may provoke sinusitis.

Maintain Breast Health

Since Cancer is the sign of the mother, it's not surprising that breasts are under its domain. If you're prone to fibrocystic breast condition, dietary strategies can be of great benefit. Eliminating (or at least reducing) caffeine and limiting saturated fat–rich foods like red meat can help with breast tenderness. In addition to regularly scheduled gynecological appointments, monthly self-exams are an important strategy for early breast cancer detection. If you have issues with your breasts—their size and/or shape—you're not alone. While many women wish their breasts were different, the first step in taking the best care of your breasts is to appreciate them—and the beauty of their uniqueness—as they are.

Reduce Water Retention

Not only do Cancerians cling tightly to their feelings and possessions (and the past), but your body may also hold on to excess water. To curb a tendency toward swelling and bloating, avoid overly salty foods and drink adequate amounts of filtered water. As potassium helps with fluid balance, make sure you get adequate amounts of this mineral through your diet. Vegetables and fruits—especially leafy greens, melons, citrus fruit, and, of course, bananas—are among the best choices because they provide you with the greatest amount of potassium per calorie.

 HEALTHY EATING TIPS

Cancerians gravitate toward food; after all, yours is the sign of nourishment and nurturance. While food can provide you with comfort, be aware of becoming too reliant on it for soothing wistful moods.

Be Aware of Emotional Eating

Cancerians equate the act of eating with the act of being nurtured. Food can feed the Cancerian soul, and eating is part of your self-soothing repertoire. But therein lies the rub: as sensitive Cancerians frequently look for consolation, emotional eating often leads to overeating.

★ There is nothing inherently wrong with feeling nurtured by food—in fact, experiencing a sense of comfort from your meals is an integral facet of fostering well-being. It's just important to avoid using food as a panacea for your problems. If you find yourself eating to soothe anxiety or to satisfy an oral fixation, instead try chewing gum or snacking on carrots, celery, or other low-calorie, healthy finger food.

Lovingly Prepare Your Food

The Crab loves to cook. For you, it's not just that home is where the heart is; the heart is where the hearth is. So nurture your body while you nurture your spirit by cooking your own meals whenever you can. As you cook, focus on the food, infusing it with the abundant love you carry in your heart to further enhance the nourishing comfort it can provide you.

★ Cooking your own meals doesn't mean having to spend a lot of time in the kitchen. There are many cookbooks available that can help you prepare quick, easy, and healthy meals in a matter of minutes. When you do go to restaurants, see if you can meet the chef, or at least peek in the kitchen to see who's cooking, as it can help you feel more connected to your food.

Cook with Your Melting Pot

As a Crab, your sense of security is closely tied to your family tree. The past, including who and what came before you, provides you with a strong sense of rootedness. Nurture this link to your lineage by taking a cooking class or buying cookbooks based on meals from your ethnic background or cultural heritage. In addition, consider compiling a collection of your family's favorite old-world recipes.

★ A trip to an ethnic food market can help you find ingredients as well as a piece of your cultural identity. Conversations with store owners may give you additional insights into traditional recipes and cooking methods. If there aren't any ethnic food markets in your neighborhood, a simple Internet search will turn up resources where you can purchase specialty ingredients.

HEALTH-SUPPORTING FOODS

Included among the most nourishing foods for the Crab are cancer-preventative brassica vegetables and heart-healthy soy foods. Often looking for foods with soothing textures, a Cancerian may appreciate Moon-ruled summer and winter squash.

Brassica Vegetables

Family is important to a Cancerian, and the *Brassica* family of vegetables—including broccoli, cabbage, cauliflower, watercress, and mustard greens—can be important to your health. Also known as *crucifers*, their unique sulfur-containing nutrients help the liver neutralize cancer-causing chemicals. This could help explain why research has shown that women who regularly eat brassica vegetables have a lower risk of developing breast cancer.

★ Steamed broccoli or cauliflower drizzled with extra virgin olive oil and a touch of lemon juice makes a quick-and-easy side dish. Watercress and mizuna (Japanese mustard greens) are great additions to salads. Sauerkraut and the Korean staple, kimchi, are delicious cabbage-based dishes.

Soy Foods

While soy foods may not be the magic bullet that some claim them to be, they are versatile and tasty diet additions with health benefits that should not be discounted. Soy foods help promote bone health and lower cholesterol and, if consumed during adolescence, are thought to reduce breast cancer risk.

★ To get the most from soy foods, enjoy them as they're consumed in Asia, where they're prepared with traditional fermentation processes and eaten in moderation. Eat whole soy foods—such as tofu, tempeh, miso, and natto—rather than isolated soy-derived ingredients, like soy protein isolate and texturized vegetable protein. Look for products made with organic soybeans, which are GMO-free.

Squash

Squash is a Cancerian, Moon-ruled food that you can enjoy all year long. Summer squash, including zucchini, is low in calories and very filling. Winter squash features a comforting creamy texture and a sweetness that will help curb sugar cravings.

★ Summer squash is wonderful raw as crudités or sautéed as a delicious side dish. Experiment with the many varieties of winter squash including kabocha, sugar pumpkin, and delicata in addition to the old standbys of acorn and butternut. Steaming is a quick way to cook winter squash, and cutting it into small cubes reduces the cooking time to less than ten minutes.

SPA AND WELLNESS THERAPIES

Spa and wellness therapies nurture your body and soothe your soul. Treatments that involve bathing provide a nourishing sense of aquatic cocooning precious to the Crab.

Hydrotherapy

Just like your totem, the sea-dwelling Crab, water is the *prima materia* of your being. So why not soak up the many health benefits of this fundamental elixir by treating yourself to a hydrotherapy session? Also known as *balneotherapy*, hydrotherapy is a catch-all phrase for healing treatments—such as underwater massages and mineral-rich soaking tubs—that involve water.

★ Many spas offer Vichy shower treatments, letting you add a touch of hydrotherapy to any service you enjoy. During this treatment, you lie on a massage table while water gently rains down on you from several overhead shower jets.

Milk Bath

Take Cleopatra's lead and enjoy a luxurious skin-softening milk bath, a beauty ritual for which she was known. During this nurturing spa treatment, you soak in a tub filled with milk- and flower-infused water or have warmed milk poured over your body as you lie on a massage table (the benefits of this body treatment are thought to come from the milk's lactic acid, which gently exfoliates your skin). A milk bath is often followed by a body wrap, in which you're swaddled in herb-laden linens and left to rest and regenerate.

★ You can do a modified version of this treatment at home. Add a cup of warmed milk and a few drops of your favorite floral essential oil—or a sachet of powdered milk and flower petals—to your bath water.

Java Lulur

Java lulur is a spa treatment tailor-made for a Cancerian; it is utterly feminine, incorporates the Cancer-ruled jasmine flower, and is steeped in tradition. This decadent therapy features a jasmine oil massage followed by a body scrub that includes jasmine, turmeric, and rice bran. After that, you're treated to a honey and yogurt body scrub and then a flower petal bath. While Java lulur is a time-honored ritual experienced by Indonesian brides-to-be, you needn't be prenuptial to enjoy its delights.

★ Different spas have their own take on Java lulur, interpreting this ritual in a variety of ways. Inquire about the spa's offerings (including time and cost) before booking a treatment session.

RELAXATION PRACTICES

Cancerians can increase their state of peace by making time to nurture themselves, rather than just others, doing whatever it is that most pacifies their soul.

Regularly Scheduled "Me Time"

Just like the Crab, which requires a quiet, undisturbed environment to molt and rejuvenate itself, you also need respites of peace and solitude to foster inner growth. It's important to carve out regular time away from attending to the needs of others so you can focus on yourself and do the things that you love to do. Take a day (or even a few hours) off and laze in the bath, try out a new recipe, read a trashy novel, or whatever floats your Cancerian boat.

★ While many crabs molt every few months, you probably need to enjoy revitalizing "me days" a little more often. As Cancerians are so in tune with lunar cycles, why not schedule your personal retreats at the new and/or full moon.

Genealogy Projects

Your sign's deep connection to the past is an intricate part of your identity. To better understand your roots, why not dig up information on your ancestors and create a family tree? Talking to older relatives is a great place to start. Inquire about statistics—names, places, and dates—and also gather stories. For the nostalgic Cancerian, the sentimental nature of genealogy can bring on a state of peace.

★ A vast amount of genealogy resources are available on the Internet. In addition to the numerous websites that will help you search through public records, there are also discussion boards where you can get advice from others who are also navigating their ancestry.

Aquatic Fitness Classes

For a Crab, exercising in your natural habitat of the water can be very relaxing. Aquatic fitness classes provide an opportunity for a cardiovascular workout that's safe, stress-free, and low impact—just the way a Cancerian likes things. Moving against the resistance of the water, you build flexibility, endurance, and joint health. Aquatic fitness classes are designed for an array of energy and ability levels, so you will surely find one that best suits your needs.

★ Most gyms or community centers with swimming pools offer a range of aquatic fitness classes. If you're not an avid swimmer, don't worry—in most classes, you usually wear flotation belts.

YOGA POSES

Yoga can be a gentle form of exercise that offers benefits for Cancer-related body parts such as the sinuses and stomach. As is done in certain traditions, consider not practicing yoga on the new and full moons.

Standing Forward Bend (*Uttanasana*)

In addition to stretching the hips, hamstrings, and calves, Standing Forward Bend is good for enhancing the health of the Cancer-ruled sinuses and stomach. It's often referred to as "waterfall pose," well suited to your aqueous nature.

★ Stand tall with your feet together and your hands on your hips. Bend forward at your hips (not at your waist). Bring your fingertips or palms to the floor in front of your feet. Keep your legs straight without locking your knees. If the floor or your ankles are not within reach, bend your knees slightly, let your arms hang down, and grab opposite elbows, crossing your forearms. Regardless of your arm position, let your head hang down. Remain in the pose for up to one minute. To rise, roll up through your spine one vertebra at a time.

Easy Pose with Alternate Nostril Breathing (*Sukhasana/Nadi Sodhana*)

Easy Pose is a calming seated posture, wonderful in and of itself, and one that you can also use for meditation. Alternate nostril breathing is helpful in preventing sinus infections. It is also deeply relaxing and helps to center the emotions.

★ Sit on the edge of a folded blanket that is four to six inches high. Crossing shins, open your knees to the side with your feet underneath opposite knees, and let your knees and outer legs fall toward the floor. Press your right thumb on your right nostril to close it. Inhale through your left nostril for four counts. Close your left nostril with your right ring finger, release your thumb, and exhale through your right nostril for four counts. Inhale through your right nostril for four counts, and then close it with your thumb. Simultaneously release hold on your left nostril and exhale for four counts. Continue for twelve rounds or more.

Legs-Up-the-Wall Pose (*Viparita Karani*)

This gentle, restorative pose inspires calm and relaxation, helps with Cancerian water retention, and can move blood through the stomach and reproductive organs. This allows you to gain the many benefits offered by other inversion postures without the intensity and stress they may cause.

★ Sit on the floor with the right side of your body next to a wall and your legs bent and feet on the floor. Lie down so you are in a modified fetal position. Pivot yourself so you are lying on the ground. Straighten your legs and rest them on the wall, scooting your buttocks forward so that they are as close to the wall as possible. Close your eyes and relax for at least five minutes.

 AROMATHERAPY

That a flower, fruit, or herb is able to not only promote physical well-being but also elicit positive sentiments—from the joyful to the tranquil—is sure to please a sensitive Cancerian.

Jasmine (*Jasminum officinale*)

Jasmine is a flower governed by your planetary ruler, the Moon. Given that its sweet and intoxicating fragrance grows stronger as night falls and the Moon rises, its lunar relationship is not surprising. A powerful aphrodisiac, jasmine can help you open more deeply to your Cancerian nurturing instincts while its rapturous scent can help lift your mood.

★ Enjoy the seductive fragrance of jasmine by wearing it as a natural perfume. Use jasmine-scented oil for a sensual couple's massage. If straight jasmine essential oil is not in your budget, a more affordable variety, diluted with jojoba oil, will also bring you joy.

Hyssop (*Hyssop decumbens*)

Hyssop essential oil can help if your digestion needs a little jump start or if you retain water during your period (or other times of the month). It's known as an "herb of protection," thought to help fortify the boundaries of those—like the Crab—who absorb other people's worries and stress. And for tradition-loving Cancerians, it's nice to know that hyssop has been around for a long time, reflected by its mention in the Bible as an herb associated with purification.

★ Use hyssop in a room diffuser to cleanse the air, especially if someone in your house is sick. Hyssop mixed with massage oil makes a great belly balm for upset stomachs or water retention. While several types of hyssop are available, make sure to purchase the *decumbens* variety as others contain compounds that may be unhealthy.

Clary Sage (*Salvia sclarea*)

Clary sage is a classic essential oil for women, used to relieve menstrual cramps as well as menopausal symptoms such as hot flashes. It is well known for its sweet and euphoric fragrance, which elevates moods and centers emotions. As its name suggests, it provides you with the wisdom of clarity, both in thoughts and in feelings.

★ Clary sage is a wonderful essential oil to use during that time of the month. Add some to your body lotion, and rub it onto your belly to alleviate the cramps and bloating that can accompany menstruation. A warm bath with a few drops of clary sage creates an enchanting relaxation ritual.

 NATURAL REMEDIES

As the sign associated with the mother, it makes sense to a Cancerian that Mother Nature can yield healing treasures.

Vitex (*Vitex agnus-castus*)

The Moon reflects the archetype of cycles, which are so intimately tied to femininity. Therefore, it's no wonder that your planetary ruler, the Moon, rules vitex, one of the premier herbs for woman's health. Well regarded in Europe as a remedy for premenstrual syndrome, vitex is also used to reduce fibrocystic breast tenderness, combat menopausal symptoms, and even promote regular ovulatory cycles and fertility.

★ While vitex helps to regulate hormone balance, it is actually hormone-free. It's also known as chasteberry, reflecting the traditional belief that it inspired chastity by reducing sexual drive (don't worry, there's been no research to support such a claim).

De-Glycyrrhizinated Licorice (*Glycyrrhiza glabra*)

De-glycyrrhizinated licorice (DGL) is a dietary supplement made from licorice. Its "de-glycyrrhizinated" prefix reflects that it is free of glycyrrhizin, a natural licorice component that can cause water retention and increase blood pressure. DGL can benefit a Cancerian in need of some stomach soothing, as it curbs indigestion and heartburn. Research suggests that it may heal stomach ulcers as well as aphthous ulcers, the latter being a fancy name for the not-so-fancy canker sore.

★ As DGL needs to be in contact with saliva to work, this supplement comes in chewable wafer form. Some companies sell DGL wafers that are flavored, a boon for those who don't like the taste of licorice.

Bromelain

As bromelain helps break down protein, these supplements are used as digestive aids and help to alleviate heartburn. Bromelain has also been found to relieve symptoms of acute sinusitis. Since it also addresses many other ailments—including joint inflammation—bromelain is a great remedy to keep in your medicine cabinet.

★ If you use bromelain supplement as a digestive aid, take it with meals. For other uses, it is best to take it on an empty stomach. As a way to ensure potency, look for bromelain supplements that report MUCs or GDUs (units of activity) rather than just milligrams.

 FLOWER ESSENCES

Flower essences, subtle remedies that work to balance emotional well-being, can help Cancerians connect to their deep well of feelings, the source of their vital strength. All flower essences can be used similarly: mix a few drops in a glass of water, and drink several times a day; add some to a bath; or place in a water-filled mister bottle to enhance your environment.

Baby Blue Eyes (*Nemophila menziesii*)

Like your astrological symbol, the Crab, you likely have a hard protective shell. Your defensive veneer helps you, an über-sensitive soul, to feel safe when you venture into the world. Yet this armor can sometimes keep you away from what you most crave: emotional connections with others. Baby Blue Eyes flower essence can help enhance your belief in your amazing intuitive nature, allowing you to let down your guard while still feeling protected.

Clematis (*Clematis vitalba*)

As a daydreamy Cancerian, you may sometimes appear to be "here"—present to the world around you—while you're actually "there"—burrowed in the feelings that reside within. While this withdrawal into the shell of your vivid internal life may appeal to your sensitive nature, it can sometimes keep you from facing tasks and achieving goals. When you need to bolster your ability to stay present within yourself and yet actively interact with the world, try Clematis flower essence.

Honeysuckle (*Lonicera caprifolium*)

Cancerians are nostalgic. The reliability of what came before gives you security, and the sense of being connected to your personal roots gives you comfort. While it's important to honor the past, a Crab may also have a tendency to get stuck in it, which can pull you away from truly living in the present. If you need a little help removing the pincer grip of the past, try Honeysuckle flower essence.

leo

SUN IN LEO ★ July 23–August 22

CHARACTERISTICS ★ Self-expressive / Magnanimous /
Proud / Self-focused / Faithful / Forthright / Charismatic /
Courageous / Cheerful / Dignified / Winsome / Dramatic

SYMBOL ★ The *Lion*, an animal known for its lustrous mane
and magnificent roar. As king of the jungle, the Lion is territorial,
fierce, and powerful. In mythological and cultural traditions, the
Lion is a symbol of strength, bravery, creation, and royalty.

PLANETARY RULER ★ The *Sun*, a star at the center of our
solar system that radiates heat and around which all planets orbit.
The god of the Sun in both Greek and Roman mythology was
Apollo, who governed truth, prophecy, and healing. In astrology,
the Sun represents the creative life force and the vital essence
of who a person is.

ELEMENT ★ *Fire*, characterized by the dynamic energy
of inspiration, enthusiasm, and passion. It is transformative,
kinetic, and action oriented.

QUALITY ★ *Fixed*, which represents the planning and building
phase of the creative cycle. It reflects reliability, predictability,
and a disciplined force that persists in creating structure.

PERSONAL HEALTH PROFILE

A Leo radiates an incandescent sense of wellness and vivacity. Roaring with stamina, you energetically participate in the many experiences life presents to you, including those that allow you to share your creative and shining self with the world.

Yet with an ambitious and generous spirit, you may become overly fired up about the projects you undertake, which can sometimes be stressful, let alone exhausting. Luckily, that fiery nature and ability to find creative solutions will usually help you quickly rebound to your full-spirited energy level.

While Leos have an active and enthusiastic nature, it's important to recognize that you can sometimes fall prey to streaks of laziness. Let yourself enjoy these respites, although be aware if they cause you to stray too far from your dedication to exercise, eating well, and other aspects of your wellness routine.

The motivation of Leos to continually better themselves, in addition to their desire to take control of their own destinies, makes a self-care program of wellness therapies and natural remedies very attractive. Self-care lets you rely on your strong sense of agency rather than having to depend on others, thus allowing you to maintain the dignity so important to the proud Leonine soul.

Another reason Leos so willingly engage in self-care is that wellness therapies are enjoyable, especially the ones that involve pampering. What Leo doesn't love a day at the spa? You get to enhance your health and enjoy the treasures of sybaritic pleasure, all the while having someone lavish you with special attention. Being queen or king for a day (or even a few hours) is something to which regal Leos are drawn.

While Leos like to be in charge, when you do fall ill, it's important not to let your pride get in the way of asking for help.

For a Leo, the ideal health-care practitioner is someone who will treat you as an individual—not just another patient—and who will respect you and your opinion. As a confident and engaged Leo, you should make sure your health-care provider shines full attention on you (without being patronizing) so you can feel secure and best taken care of.

 ## AREAS OF HEALTH FOCUS

Each zodiac sign is associated with certain parts of the body. These may be inherent areas of vulnerability, but when attended to, they can become areas of strength. The parts of the body associated with Leo include the following:

★ The **heart**, which keeps blood flowing and symbolizes love and joy

★ The **spine**, through which vital life-force energy flows

★ The **hair**, an expression of your luster

Your Leonine creativity, courage, and ability to express yourself are some of the resources you can use when facing any health challenge.

Care for Your Heart

Since the sign of Leo rules the heart, Lions need to pay particular attention to their cardiovascular health. High blood pressure and atherosclerosis can cause your heart to work harder than it needs to. Your self-motivation is a plus here, as an individually guided wellness program of exercise, diet, and stress management practices can do wonders for heart health. Also important is being true to your Leonine nature: the Lion has a vast reservoir of love and affection, and by expressing your warm and generous nature, you can help keep your heart in regal condition.

Support Your Back

The spine not only holds you up and gives you shape but it is also thought to be the channel through which vital life-force energy flows. With Leo ruling the spine, the potential for back issues may be front and center in a Lion's life. As Leo is a fixed sign, maintaining flexibility—in both body and mind—is important and beneficial for those born under this sign. Look to yoga or similar forms of exercise to keep your back muscles supple (and your heart peaceful). If you have chronic back pain, movement-repatterning approaches—such as the Alexander Technique or Feldenkrais Method—may be very beneficial.

Maintain Your Glorious Mane

Lions are known for their manes, their noble crowns of hair, which communicate their prowess and stature. Similarly, as a Leo, your hair is likely to be one of the features you shower with a lot of attention and take great care in maintaining. While hair and scalp health require a range of nutrients, three key ones are protein, omega-3 fatty acids, and the B vitamin biotin. For a lustrous mane, regularly massage your scalp and deep condition your hair. And, as another reason to avoid stress, know that it can negatively impact your hair, as can certain medications and excessive alcohol intake.

Get Some Sun

Sunshine is vital for a Leo's health. Your body is like one large solar cell, needing the rays of the Sun to charge your internal energy generator. So when the Sun doesn't shine—say, during the winter or in cloudy environs—you may be prone to seasonal affective disorder, appropriately called SAD. These wintertime blues are characterized by low energy, mood lulls, and carbohydrate cravings. If spending winter in Hawaii just isn't an option, don't despair. Full-spectrum lighting, regular exercise, vitamin D supplements, and just getting out into the fresh air can do wonders for your emotional and physical health.

HEALTHY EATING TIPS

Leos enjoy life, and food and drink can definitely add to your pleasure; the challenge, of course, is not going overboard with overindulgences that can compromise your waistline and well-being.

Eat Heart-Healthy Foods

To keep your arteries in top-notch shape, limit foods high in saturated fats—such as red meat—and shy away from synthetic transfatty acids found in hydrogenated oils. Some beneficial foods for heart health include omega-3–rich fish as well as nuts and seeds bursting with vitamin E and phytosterols. And, of course, enjoy an array of colorful fiber-rich fruits and vegetables, essential for cardiovascular health.

★ For a meal to be heart healthy, avoid having saturated fat–rich meat play the leading role. Instead, let small portions (four to six ounces) costar on your plate with vegetables and whole grains. Create salads with a range of colored vegetables to enjoy a palette of different health-promoting phytonutrients.

Balance Out Your Fiery Energy

As the sign associated with the Sun, Leos burn hot. In Ayurvedic medicine, a fiery constitution is known as *pitta*. When *pitta* becomes excessive, it can manifest in skin rashes, stomach acidity, inflammation, excess body heat, and irritability. If you find yourself overheating and faced with a short fuse, consider a cooling diet to balance excess *pitta*.

★ Grapes and melon are very cooling, as are zucchini, cucumbers, broccoli, sprouts, and mint. While it may seem counterintuitive, avoid iced drinks if you have a fiery constitution; according to Ayurvedic medicine, too much cold can extinguish beneficial digestive fire, which can lead to indigestion and nutrient malabsorption.

Celebrate in Moderation

Leos love parties; after all, they're an opportunity for fun, one of your favorite pastimes. Yet parties—with their abundance of cocktails and canapés—can be challenging to your diet. It's easy to be so involved in meeting and greeting that you don't realize how much you eat.

★ Enjoying a few drinks sans alcohol will save you calories and won't dampen your fire the next morning. If sparkling water seems too dull, try a festive nonalcoholic "mocktail" instead. A light preparty snack can curb your appetite and help you make nonimpulsive food choices.

Many delicious foods can help support the health of the Leo-ruled heart. Not surprising, in medical astrology, some of these—including grapes and the eponymous sunflower seeds—happen to be governed by your planetary ruler, the Sun.

Grapes

Like a Leo, grapes need plenty of sunshine to flourish. Among their numerous benefits, grapes are a sweet way to keep your heart in tip-top shape. While green grapes are delicious, red and purple ones contain more antioxidants, including the polyphenol resveratrol (which is even more concentrated in red wine). This nutrient extraordinaire is a hot topic in research circles for its cardiovascular and anti-aging benefits.

★ Grapes make a delicious snack and are particularly refreshing when frozen. While red wine may offer cardiovascular benefits, it only does so when enjoyed in moderation. If you want to steer clear of alcohol, enjoy grape juice or dealcoholized wine instead.

Sunflower Seeds

Not surprisingly, the sunflower—with its halo of brilliant yellow petals—is ruled by the Sun in medical astrology. The seeds of this majestic flower are one of the most concentrated food sources of vitamin E, which, by protecting LDL cholesterol from oxidization, can help reduce the development of atherosclerosis. Sunflower seeds are also rich in phytosterols, plant-based nutrients that can lower cholesterol levels.

★ Add sunflower seeds to salads, cereals, and stir-fries. Try a heart-healthy SB&J sandwich made from sunflower seed butter and orange marmalade. While they may make a good snack, moderation is key since sunflower seeds contain about 400 calories per half cup.

Omega-3–Rich Foods

A Leo's fiery constitution may create heat that exacerbates conditions of inflammation. Some of the best anti-inflammatory nutrients around are omega-3 fatty acids, which can support the health of your heart and hair, and help your skin defend against sunburn. Among the richest sources of omega-3 fatty acids are salmon, flaxseed, chia seeds, walnuts, winter squash, and the wild green purslane.

★ Top a salad of purslane and your other favorite greens with canned salmon for an easy-to-prepare lunch option. Chopped walnuts make a wonderful topping for baked winter squash. Add ground flaxseed or chia seeds to cold cereal, oatmeal, or yogurt.

 # SPA AND WELLNESS THERAPIES

Spa and wellness therapies, especially those that leave you feeling pampered and well attended to, can be a very enjoyable part of a Leo's health-care regimen.

Hot Stone Massage

Combine your fondness for being pampered with your love of lazy lion heat, and enjoy a luxurious hot stone massage. By using smooth river stones that have been heated to a comfortably hot temperature, the practitioner provides you with a muscle-relaxing

Swedish massage. The stones are also left to rest on different areas of your body—including along your spine, a special treat for Leos with back concerns. The stones' warmth melts away stress and tension, allowing the practitioner to work deeper muscles without applying a lot of pressure.

★ Although hot stone massages are a bit pricier than traditional ones, this Leonine treat is well worth it. Try a modified version of this spa therapy at home: purchase specially polished massage stones, heat them to a comfortable temperature in a pot of water, and apply them to different areas of your body.

Biofeedback

As a Leo, you have a great talent for gleaning insights from the world around you and using them for your own personal growth. That's what makes biofeedback such a great therapy for you. In a biofeedback session, body functions—such as heart rate or muscle tension—are measured and relayed back to you. Using these signals, you then focus on your intended goal—for example, relaxing your body—as you continue to receive feedback regarding your progress. Biofeedback is commonly used for alleviating hypo- or hypertension, chronic back pain, and tension headaches.

★ The Biofeedback Certification Institute of America features a list of practitioners on their website, www.bcia.affiniscape.com. To be certified by the organization, a practitioner must hold a degree in a related health field, complete course work and mentored clinical training, and pass an examination.

Hair and Scalp Treatments

As Leos hold their manes in high regard, taking good care of your hair will help you feel your best. Many spas offer treatments specifically designed to encourage the health and beauty of your hair and scalp. Consider a deeply moisturizing jojoba oil treatment or a nourishing mudpack. If your hair has been damaged from too much sun exposure, try a Hawaiian-inspired treatment of coconut and kukui nut oils. And don't forget about regular trims; it's the easiest way to take care of split ends and add sheen and luster to your locks.

★ Most spas offer hair and scalp treatments that you can enjoy alone or as an add-on to other treatments. If you don't have the time or money to make it to the spa, pamper your hair and scalp at home with regular hot oil and deep-conditioning treatments.

RELAXATION PRACTICES

Leos are most at ease when they are able to shine brightly, expressing the warmth of their hearts and sharing their dynamic selves with the world.

Sunbathing

For Leos, relaxing is simple: a beach chair, a book, and the Sun's warming rays are the perfect recipe for melting away stress. If you can't get out into the Sun, bring it—or at least a close approximation of it—to you. Consider getting a light box or brightening up your home and/or office by using full-spectrum lightbulbs.

★ While ultraviolet rays will recharge your spirit, it's still important to practice good sunbathing habits. Invest in sunglasses with UV protection, and don't forget to wear an SPF lotion; after all, sunburns are anything but relaxing. Full-spectrum bulbs come in an array of styles that fit most every type of lighting fixture.

Child's Play

Your playful Leonine spirit makes you a natural with kids. Spending time with children will remind you of how fun and uncomplicated life can be. It also helps you reconnect with your inner child and the zest that comes from seeing things with fresh, unadulterated eyes, allowing your heart to shine even more brightly.

★ If you don't have kids of your own—or even if you do—consider volunteering with a children's organization. For example, many schools and nonprofits have programs through which you can academically tutor children or coach them in intramural sports.

Acting

For you, Leo, the world is your stage, and every life event is an opportunity to be true to your passionately expressive nature. So why not tap further into your inner thespian—or drama queen— and take acting classes. Not only will you learn skills that will help you dig deeper into your essential creativity, but you'll have a lot of fun to boot. Acting classes offer a structured venue for being in the spotlight, enabling you to feel safe and supported, something Leos need to most brightly shine.

★ Acting teachers have different styles, methods of teaching, and of course, personalities. See whether you can visit several different classes before committing to one.

 **YOGA POSES**

Yoga can help Leos circulate radiant heat and energy throughout their bodies. Poses that focus on the heart, circulatory system, and spine can be particularly beneficial.

Lion Pose (*Simhasana*)

Lion Pose will help you to embody the inherent courage and fearlessness that reside in every Leo's heart. This playful posture encourages self-expression while it exercises your throat and eyes.

★ Kneel on the floor with your heels facing upward and pressed against your buttocks. With your fingers spread wide, place your palms on your knees. Inhale through your nose and exhale through your mouth, opening it wide. Stick out your tongue, reaching it down toward your chin, and loudly make the sound "ha." Simultaneously, look up and lightly focus your eyes above the bridge of your nose. Repeat several times.

Cat Pose (*Marjaryasana*)

Another feline-inspired posture is Cat Pose, which gently opens up your middle back and creates more space for your heart. It helps warm up the spine and massages your digestive organs without creating excess heat.

★ Place your hands and knees on the floor in the tabletop position (your knees should align directly below your hips, with your elbows and wrists below your shoulders). Your neck should be in a neutral position with your eyes gazing toward the floor. Exhale, and while keeping your shoulders and knees in position, round your back toward the ceiling. Release your head between your arms so the crown of your head points toward the floor. Hold for several seconds. Inhale, moving your spine back to the tabletop position for several seconds. Repeat the sequence eight to twelve times.

Sphinx Pose

In ancient Egypt, the sphinx—the mythological lion-bodied creature—was heralded as the temple guardian. Practicing the chest-opening Sphinx Pose can help safeguard your very own temple, that of your heart.

★ Lie facedown on your mat, with your feet hip distance apart and the tops of your feet touching the floor. Focus on keeping your legs grounded into the mat by pressing down through your pinky toe and lengthening out through your feet. Place your elbows directly under your shoulders, with your arms resting on the mat straight in front of you and your fingers spread wide. Push down through your forearms so your torso lifts into a mini-backbend. Make sure to move your shoulder blades down your back. Focus on lengthening your spine and not compressing your lower back by pulling in your abdominal muscles. Stay in the posture for several breaths.

AROMATHERAPY

Leos like to express their individuality, and using fragrant essential oils as perfumes is one way to do so.

Neroli (*Citrus aurantium*)

Neroli is derived from the flower blossoms of the Seville orange tree. Like the sign of Leo, neroli is associated with nobility, named after the seventeenth-century princess who first made it popular. This regal oil—with its sweetly floral scent—makes a wonderful perfume. Its fragrance is very calming, helping to inspire joy and banish restlessness. It's also said to have cooling properties and is therefore used for conditions of excess heat, including high blood pressure.

★ Soak in neroli's aromatic essence by sprinkling some in a hot bath. Dab a few drops of neroli oil on your heart and wear as a perfume. Add some to body lotion for enhanced circulation.

Lemon (*Citrus limon*)

Like a Leo, lemon essential oil is bright and cheery and makes people smile. The happiness elicited by lemon isn't solely due to its uplifting fragrance, but also because of the many health benefits it provides. Lemon essential oil adds shine to the hair and cleanses the scalp. It's known as one of the best "blood movers," improving sluggish circulation, mending broken capillaries, and reducing blood pressure.

★ Use lemon oil in a diffuser to lend an incandescent energy to a room. Lemon-scented body oil is uplifting and refreshing. Don't apply lemon oil straight to the skin, especially if you will be in the sun, as it can cause photosensitivity.

German Chamomile (*Matricaria recutita*)

German chamomile is a powerful example of the transformative energy of fire, the element that inspires the Leonine spirit. The heat used to distill the oil from the flower creates a new compound, chamazulene, well known for its powerful anti-inflammatory properties and deep blue color. German chamomile is used to alleviate red, dry, and irritated skin. Its applelike floral scent is soothing yet uplifting.

★ Add some German chamomile to a clay face mask to unmask your skin's true radiance. A few drops in a warm bath or used as a perfume will inspire a sunny and peaceful mood. Avoid German chamomile if you have an allergy to ragweed, as you'll likely be sensitive to it as well.

NATURAL REMEDIES

Leos like to be in charge, and using natural remedies provides you with another way to manage your well-being routine.

Vitamin D

Vitamin D is known as the "sunshine vitamin" because the Sun's ultraviolet rays make it active in our bodies. Anything that causes reduced Sun exposure—such as staying indoors, living in a cloudy climate, or wearing protective clothing—can put people at risk for vitamin D deficiency. Vitamin D is a hot topic in nutrition research: once famous solely for its contribution to bone density, it is now thought to play a role in heart health and in the alleviation of depression.

★ Vitamin D supplements are available in either D2 or D3 form. The former is from plant or yeast sources while the latter is often derived from sheep's wool. To determine the optimal amount for you to supplement, ask your doctor about tests that can measure your vitamin D levels.

St. John's Wort (*Hypericum perforatum*)

The sun-colored St. John's wort flower is a remedy traditionally associated with Leo and your planetary ruler, the Sun. Most famously known for treating mild depression, St. John's wort may also benefit those who experience seasonal affective disorder, the blues that occur from a lack of sun exposure. A salve made from this healing herb can be used topically for calming sunburns as well as relieving bruises and skin irritations.

★ St. John's wort is available in capsule, liquid tincture, or topical form. In some individuals, taking St. John's wort may cause photosensitivity (sun allergy), resulting in itching and redness.

Chamomile (*Matricaria recutita*)

Considering that its bright yellow flower head is surrounded by a corona of petals, it's not surprising that medical astrologers associate chamomile with the Sun. Owing to its muscle relaxant and antispasmodic properties, one of its traditional uses has been as a stomach soother. And when you feel overly agitated, either during the day or before sleep, you'll appreciate the calm it can impart. Applied topically in the form of a salve or ointment, it may speed up the healing of skin irritations and rashes, and treat symptoms of eczema.

★ While chamomile can be found in capsule and liquid tincture form, it is commonly prepared as a tea using the dried flowers. If you have an allergy to ragweed, you may want to avoid chamomile since it is in the same botanical family.

FLOWER ESSENCES

Flower essences are created by placing blossoms in water and having the heat of the Sun, that which nourishes the Leo's spirit, alchemically draw out the flower's healing energies into the liquid. All flower essences can be used similarly: mix a few drops in a glass of water, and drink several times a day; add some to a bath; or place in a water-filled mister bottle to enhance your environment.

Borage (*Borago officinalis*)

The quest of Leos is to live through their hearts, expressing warmth and love to themselves and those around them. Sometimes, though, being openhearted can be challenging; for example, it's hard to be emotionally buoyant when sadness and grief rest heavy in your heart. If you want some help in fortifying your courage, especially when feeling disheartened, try Borage flower essence.

Indian Paintbrush (*Castilleja miniata*)

Born under the sign that represents self-expression, Leos are known as very creative people. You like artistic activities that allow you to show the world who you are and to be admired for the talents you embody. Yet, like all artists, you will likely experience times when your energy feels stuck and your creative juices are blocked. Indian Paintbrush flower essence can replenish your energy so that your creative visions can more readily manifest.

Sunflower (*Helianthus annuus*)

With the Sun ruling Leo, you have a powerful ability to radiate your luminous essence into the world. Harnessing that inner solar fire requires a harmonious alliance with your masculine side, the part of your personality that helps you assert yourself and feel confident. Without this connection, low self-esteem or heightened self-glory can manifest, dimming the brilliance of your powerful self-expression. Sunflower flower essence can help you bolster your solar energy, allowing your warmth and light to flourish.

virgo

SUN IN VIRGO ★ August 23–September 22

CHARACTERISTICS ★ Analytical / Skeptical / Productive / Perfectionistic / Detailed / Rational / Critical / Methodical / Anxious / Insightful / Obsessive / Service oriented

SYMBOL ★ The *Virgin*, a symbol of purity and self-sufficiency. She is often depicted holding a sheaf of grain, representing her association with fertility, agriculture, and the harvested wisdom that comes with diligent work. In mythological and cultural traditions, the Virgin is a symbol of sacred commitment, martyrdom, and the priestesses who tend the eternal flame.

PLANETARY RULER ★ *Mercury*, which has the fastest orbit around the Sun. Mercury was the Roman god of commerce, known for his role as the messenger of the gods. His counterpart in Greek mythology was Hermes. In astrology, Mercury represents communication, intellect, language, and bridge building.

ELEMENT ★ *Earth*, characterized by the grounded energy of creativity, resistance, and practicality. It is fertile and passive, and it relates to the world on a sensual level.

QUALITY ★ *Mutable*, which represents the adjustment and finessing stage of the creative cycle. It reflects flexibility, tolerance, and an adaptive and transformative free-flowing force.

Virgo is the most health-conscious sign of the zodiac, with natives diligently focused on being well and staying well. Yet, since Virgoans are perfectionists, your idea of wellness is a bit more exacting than others (after all, yours is the sign of the Virgin, making purity an enduring Virgoan goal). While someone else may accept a little ache or pain as one of life's trifles, not you. Detail-oriented Virgoans are hyperaware of all their body's signs and signals. If anything seems even slightly amiss, you notice it and want to fix it. Your analytical mind immediately springs into action, seeking a remedy to the problem so that you can readily restore your sense of well-being.

While your keen sense of analysis and your critical eye may help you solve many health-care problems, these traits may, at times, also exacerbate them. Your vigilance about your body, combined with your unswerving desire to have everything just right, can lead to undue worry. As your mind and body are particularly in sync, the resulting anxiety may not only impact your mental outlook but also disturb your physical health. It's important for a Virgoan to understand that in health, as in life, perfection is an unrealistic goal; it's not that *you* can't achieve it—it's that it just can't be achieved. Striving toward a more accepting outlook that allows for the existence of imperfections can do wonders for your sense of well-being and, ultimately, your physical health.

As the earth sign associated with the harvest, an important part of a Virgoan's wellness regimen is centered on diet. Since a Virgoan appreciates the bounty of the land, the joys and health benefits of organic and natural foods are probably nothing new to you.

Your ideal health-care practitioner understands the inextricable link between mind and body. Whatever their scope of practice, you want them to be masters of their craft. Ideally, they are able to communicate both the general concepts and details of health maintenance; this way, you can better understand how their recommendations fit together as practical steps for your attainment of optimal health.

AREAS OF HEALTH FOCUS

Each zodiac sign is associated with certain parts of the body. These may be inherent areas of vulnerability, but when attended to, they can become areas of strength. The parts of the body associated with Virgo include the following:

★ The **small intestine**, an organ of digestion that absorbs many nutrients

★ The **pancreas**, which produces digestive enzymes

★ The **gall bladder**, which stores bile, necessary to break down fats

Your Virgoan critical-thinking skills, keen physical awareness, and perceptive mind are some of the resources you can use when facing any health challenge.

Aid Digestion

Discern and *assimilate* are two key words used to describe Virgo as well as the function of the small intestine, an organ ruled by your sign and often an area of vulnerability. As such, Virgoans may want to pay careful attention to their digestive health. Excess stress and the routine intake of aspirin and other nonsteroidal anti-inflammatory drugs (NSAIDs) can lead to intestinal permeability, a cause of indigestion and nutrient malabsorption. One way to boost intestinal health is to eat a diet rich in anti-inflammatory nutrients, including omega-3 fatty acids (featured in cold-water fish) as well as the flavonoid and carotenoid phytonutrients found concentrated in fruits and vegetables. Probiotic supplements can also be helpful as they promote the reestablishment of healthy populations of beneficial intestinal flora.

Respect Food Sensitivities

Virgoans are very discriminating: your methodical nature compels you to classify the good from the not-so-good. Combine this with the fact that your sign governs the act of digestion, and you've got a recipe for food sensitivities. In this physiological happening, your body readily judges foods as either friend or foe, with the latter triggering inflammation that can lead to nutrient malabsorption. They can also cause indigestion, depression, and headaches. If these symptoms are on your list of health complaints and the causes remain an undiagnosed mystery, you may want to investigate the possibility of adverse food reactions with your health-care practitioner.

Promote Gall Bladder Health

Traditional Chinese medicine—fond of describing the body in poetic ways—portrays the gall bladder as exacting and decisive, characteristics that also describe your sign. The gall bladder serves as the storehouse for bile. Without adequate bile, fats aren't well digested, which can lead to malabsorption and food sensitivities. The Western diet, filled with refined foods and overloaded with saturated fats, exacerbates gall bladder disturbances. As fiber-filled whole foods can promote the health of this small—but very important—organ, include a cornucopia of fruits, vegetables, whole grains, and other nutrient-rich fare in your diet.

Practice Acceptance

Virgoans are able to dissect a situation like no one else—analyzing the ins and outs of all the details. While this ability provides you with astonishing insights, it can also lead to an amazing amount of worry and anxiety when combined with your perfectionistic nature since you readily view that things just aren't the best that they can be. It's important to remember that not every situation needs remedying. Learning to accept situations and people (including yourself) just as they are—appreciating the inherent beauty that exists even if they appear flawed—will reduce your stress and enhance your mental and physical health.

 # HEALTHY EATING TIPS

As Virgo is an earth sign, those born under it have an instinctive knowledge that food can play an integral role in maintaining well-being. In fact, you were probably into "health food" long before it became a trend, let alone mainstream.

Avoid Food Triggers

Do you sense that certain foods may trigger feelings of malaise—whether they be digestive upsets or unsettling mood swings? If so, consider a modified allergy-avoidance or full-scale elimination diet to determine whether any foods you eat deplete your vitality.

★ Even just eliminating the food trigger triple threat—wheat, cow's milk, and eggs—from your diet for two weeks may do wonders for your wellness and allow you to deduce whether you are sensitive to one or more of these common food allergens. For a more detailed and methodical approach, consider pursuing an elimination diet with the guidance of a nutritionist.

Think Globally, Eat Locally

With theirs being the sign of the harvest, Virgoans are naturally connected to, and concerned about, the Earth. Empower yourself by purchasing locally grown and organic foods. Doing so can make a difference in the sustainability of the environment and in your health as organic foods are lower in pesticide residues than conventionally grown foods.

★ By shopping at local farmers' markets, you'll not only enjoy the freshest produce, meats, and dairy products, you'll also directly support the people who grow the food that nourishes you. Look for foods that are labeled as organic. Yet don't discount the wares of local farmers who may grow their food sustainably but who have decided not to incur the extra expense of getting their farms organically certified.

Watch Obsessive Eating Patterns

Health-oriented Virgoans may want to keep their tendency toward austerity and their affection for details in check. Otherwise, you may find yourself developing orthorexic habits. The term *orthorexia* signifies an obsession with the ideals of healthy eating, where a good portion of your energy is spent worrying about which foods to eat and how they will impact your health. This often occurs at the expense of life balance, the enjoyment of food, and, ironically, optimal health.

★ If you find yourself following a supposedly healthy diet that leaves you low in energy, you may want to consider whether it is really the best plan for you. Remember, food is not only a vehicle for health promotion, but it also reinforces your connection with nature, helps to connect you with community, and is something from which even ascetically inclined Virgoans can derive great pleasure.

 # HEALTH-SUPPORTING FOODS

Strongly connected to the land, Virgoans appreciate the bounty that nature yields. Whole grains, bitter greens, and the macrobiotic staple *umeboshi* pickled plum are some of the many natural foods that can support a Virgoan's health.

Whole Grains

The symbol for your sign, the Virgin, is often depicted holding onto a sheaf of grain, a food that can play a health-promoting role in a Virgoan's diet. Yet use your discriminating nature when selecting which grains to enjoy. Fiber-rich whole grains are better for you than ones that have been refined, which are stripped of many of their naturally occurring nutrients.

★ While wheat is ubiquitous in the Western diet, you may want to avoid it as your go-to grain as it's a top food allergen. Instead, try whole grains such as barley, spelt, teff, and quinoa; the latter two are great for people who are also gluten-reactive.

Bitter Greens

According to Chinese medicine, bitter flavors enhance the function of the Virgo-ruled small intestine, making bitter greens—such as dandelion greens, sorrel, and endive—a sweet addition to a Virgoan's healthful diet. These vegetables aid digestion, as their bitter compounds stimulate secretion of hydrochloric acid, digestive enzymes, and bile; the fact that they are rich in fiber is an added plus.

★ Use leafy greens as a basis for your next dinner salad. Also, try a splash of bitters, the bar condiment made from gentian and other herbs, in sparkling water for a delicious digestion-aiding aperitif.

Umeboshi

Efficient Virgoans will find much to love in *umeboshi* as this food has so many health benefits. Made from pickled ume plums, this Japanese alkalizing wonder curbs indigestion, enhances mineral absorption, and has a great reputation as a hangover remedy. Combined with well-cooked rice, it is part of a traditional Japanese recipe given to children when they're sick.

★ *Umeboshi* is available as whole plums, pureed paste, or vinegar. You can find it in natural food stores and Asian markets. With its tart-salty flavor, it can adorn steamed vegetables or add a zing to rice dishes. It's also combined with perilla leaves to make the delicious ume-shiso sushi roll.

 # SPA AND WELLNESS THERAPIES

Spa and wellness therapies that promote detoxification can offer you numerous healing rewards, allowing you to cleanse your body in pursuit of the purity that Virgoans so cherish.

Herbal Wraps

Herbal wraps are perfect for earthy Virgoans looking for a relaxing approach to detoxification. During this treatment you're swathed in herb-infused linens. The heat created by this cocooning as well as the herbs' stimulating effects help your body to release toxins. After being unwrapped, you are rinsed off and a moisturizing lotion is applied to further soften your skin.

★ If you're prone to feelings of claustrophobia, opt to keep your arms outside of the sheets. Also, ask which herbs are used in the treatment to ensure they are not ones to which you are sensitive.

Fasting

For Virgoans, a little sacrifice is a small price to pay for the reward of purity. Fasting reflects these ascetic aims by restricting your intake of food and cleansing your body of unwanted toxins. While water-only fasts are used therapeutically for a host of different conditions, a less restrictive approach to consider is the juice fast, which can also incorporate broths, fruits, and steamed vegetables.

★ While many hotel spas offer supervised fasting programs, you can also choose to do one at home under the guidance of a nutrition practitioner. Fastidious Virgoans should remember that fasting may be beneficial when done periodically, but fasting too often may not be health supportive.

Steam Baths

Traditional steam baths—such as the Russian *banya*—offer an ordered and ritualized approach to cleansing, an attribute that is certain to attract health-conscious Virgoans. At a *banya*, you alternate between sweating out toxins in a sultry steam room and cooling off by plunging into a cold pool. The heat brings blood to your skin while the cold water sends the flow of blood inward to nourish your organs.

★ Steam baths are not limited to the Russian culture; if there's no *banya* in your area, see if there's a Korean *jjimjilbang* or Turkish *hamam*. Or create your own bathing ritual at the gym, alternating between the steam room and a cold shower.

 # RELAXATION PRACTICES

Relaxation practices can help Virgoans quiet their minds, which are often sowed with worry and concern, giving them the freedom to feel at ease.

Crafting

With an eye for detail and an appreciation of functional aesthetics, Virgoans are the craftspeople of the zodiac. Channel your inner Martha—crochet scarves, design mosaic garden tiles, or refinish your bookcase. You can explore endless craft project possibilities that allow you to flex your creative muscle and relax your mind. As with all endeavors, try to temper your inner critic: instead, revel in appreciation of the unique wares you create.

★ With crafting experiencing a renaissance, there are many resources—magazines, websites, and classes—from which you can learn new skills. If your creations meet with kudos from friends and family, consider turning your hobby into a side business.

Gardening

Planting a garden and enjoying the fruits—and vegetables—of your labor can be a deliciously enriching and rewarding experience. If you don't have a yard, you can still exercise your green thumb by growing an indoor herb garden. Pots of sage, mint, and lemon balm will not only brighten your kitchen but will also add splendor to your recipes.

★ If you are new to gardening, or just need a refresher, contact the Master Gardeners in your area (www.ahs.org/master_gardeners). This community-oriented service features local volunteers who can provide you with practical tips on sustainable gardening practices.

Animal Companionship

The companionship of a dog or cat is a great antidote for stress, especially for a Virgoan, as your sign rules pets in astrology. Not only do pets happily lap up the attention you give them, but you also get something deeply nourishing for your sensitive soul in return—their healing, unconditional love.

★ Consider volunteering at your local animal shelter. You can spend time playing with the puppies or fostering rescued kittens. You get to enjoy the animals while you also get to enjoy the rewards of doing a good deed.

YOGA POSES

Yoga provides Virgoans with another way to connect with their bodies. Practicing yoga requires concentration as well as attention to detail, both traits for which Virgoans are well known.

Seated Forward Bend (*Paschimottanasana*)

While this seated posture seems simple, it provides a mindful experience of being present as you fold into yourself (if your back isn't straight, consider sitting on a folded blanket). It helps to calm anxiousness and the overanalytical Virgoan mind while toning the digestive organs.

★ Sit on the floor with your legs extended straight in front of you. Adjust your buttocks so that your sit bones are on the floor. Without locking your knees, activate your legs by pushing your thighs into the floor and extending out through your flexed feet. Inhale and lengthen your torso, and then slowly bend forward at the hips. Grab the sides of your feet, or shins, with your hands. Point your gaze toward your toes. With each inhalation, lengthen your torso, and see if you can naturally go deeper into the bend. Stay in the pose for up to two minutes.

Half Lord of the Fishes Pose (*Ardha Matsyendrasana*)

This seated spinal twist massages the intestines and stimulates digestion. During a twist you spiral around your central core—your spine—catalyzing a freer flow of energy throughout the body as well as the mind.

★ Sit on the floor with your legs extended straight in front of you. Adjust your buttocks so that your sit bones are on the floor. Bend your knees and place your feet on the floor in front of you. Slide your right foot under your left leg until your right foot is near your left hip and your right thigh is pointing straight out in front of you. Then place your left foot on the outside of your right thigh (your left knee should point up to the ceiling). Sit tall, exhale, and then twist to the left, pulling your belly in toward your spine. Place your left hand on the floor behind your left buttock, and either wrap your right arm around your left knee or place your right elbow on the outside of your left leg near your knee. Turn your head either in the direction of the twist or in the opposite direction. Stay in the pose for up to one minute.

Extended Puppy Pose (*Uttana Shishosana*)

With your sign governing pets, why not pay homage to one with your yoga practice? Extended Puppy Pose gently stretches your spine while relaxing your mind. It's a calming posture to do before sleep to help ward off insomnia.

★ Place your hands and knees on the floor in the tabletop position (your knees should align directly below your hips, with your elbows and wrists below your shoulders). Curl your toes under, and extend your arms straight out in front of you so that your forearms and palms rest on the floor. Move your buttocks back in the direction of your heels, lengthening your spine, and, as you do, resist with your arms to intensify the stretch in your back. Rest your forehead on the floor or on a folded blanket. Hold the posture for up to one minute. To come out of the pose, gently sit back on your heels.

 ## AROMATHERAPY

Since Virgoans appreciate the parts that comprise the whole, they are sure to be drawn to aromatherapy, the art of distilling fragrant essential oils from flowers, herbs, and fruits.

Melissa (*Melissa officinalis*)

Melissa and Virgoans have many things in common, not the least of which is that both are renowned for their virtues. Throughout history, the sweet-smelling melissa—also known as lemon balm—has been lauded for its many merits, including its antiviral activity and its ability to reduce anxiety and melancholy. When it comes to choosing a melissa oil, don't skimp on quality; cheaper products are often adulterated with citronella and lemongrass oils and don't feature the same benefits that pure melissa oil provides.

★ When your worries have you up late at night, a melissa-infused hot bath may help allay a tendency toward insomnia. Grow a pot of lemon balm, from which you can make a delightfully calming tea.

Cardamom (*Elletaria cardamomum*)

Cardamom essential oil is derived from the eponymous pungent and aromatic spice, widely used in Indian cuisine. Cardamom oil's warm fragrance is calming yet uplifting, and it has been used in perfume blends dating back to ancient Egypt. Well known for its aphrodisiac properties, cardamom essential oil can help disrobe Virgoan modesty that may camouflage your sexual fire.

★ Add a few drops of cardamom oil to unscented body lotion and use for a sensuality-inspiring massage. A tea made from boiled cardamom seeds mixed with honey will not only relax your mind but will also calm an upset stomach.

Carrot Seed (*Daucus carota*)

Carrot seed oil is distilled from the seed of the Mercury-ruled carrot. It is a great addition to a skin-care regimen, as it is prized for softening and rejuvenating the skin. Its liver-supporting and diuretic properties make it a great adjunct for detoxifying, a benefit certain to be appreciated by a health-conscious Virgoan.

★ Enliven your skin by mixing carrot seed oil into your moisturizer and body lotion, or add the oil to a clay mask to enhance its soothing and cleansing properties. Enjoy the detoxifying attributes, as well as earthy sweet fragrance, of carrot seed oil by adding a few drops to your bath.

NATURAL REMEDIES

Since Virgo is an earth sign, Virgoans appreciate the benefit of using natural-based substances, such as herbs and dietary supplements, to promote their well-being.

Valerian (*Valeriana officinalis*)

Medical astrologers have long associated valerian with Mercury, Virgo's ruling planet. This association makes sense given that worry-prone Virgoans may benefit from this nerve-relaxing herb. Recent studies have found that valerian may be helpful as a natural sleep aid, inducing a sense of calm that allows you to fall asleep more quickly. Unlike pharmaceutical drugs used for this purpose, valerian is nonaddictive and won't make you feel foggy the next morning.

★ While valerian offers great benefits, it has a rather off-putting smell. Consequently, valerian tea may not be the best approach; opt instead for capsules or tinctures. Valerian is often featured with other sedative herbs such as lemon balm, passionflower, and skullcap in combination herbal products.

Digestive Enzymes

When the Virgo-ruled small intestine has inadequate amounts of digestive enzymes—whether as a result of aging or eating a refined-food diet—fats, carbohydrates, and protein cannot be broken down effectively. This reduces the amount of energy you get from your food and can also lead to digestive difficulties such as bloating, gas, and heartburn. Enzyme dietary supplements can help replenish your own internal enzyme supplies, aiding in healthy digestion.

★ Many digestive enzyme supplements are plant-based, usually extracted from pineapple or papaya, or from aspergillus fungus. Yet, vegetarians may want to read the labels closely as some supplements are actually derived from animal pancreases.

Multivitamin Supplements

Virgoans take a holistic approach to life and like to cover all their bases. So consider taking a high-quality multivitamin supplement to secure the range of your nutritional needs. While not a substitute for a healthy diet, a multivitamin can be an important adjunct that ensures you're getting optimal nutrition. While they're generally called multivitamins, most also contain a gamut of minerals as well.

★ Multivitamins come in multiple forms—for example, some formulas are food-based while others are synthetically derived—so read the labels to determine which is best for you. With a multivitamin, like with everything, you get what you pay for, so spend a little more for a high-quality supplement.

 # FLOWER ESSENCES

Earth-centered Virgoans are sure to be intrigued by flower essences, elixirs of the earth that help balance emotional and psychological well-being. All flower essences can be used similarly: mix a few drops in a glass of water, and drink several times a day; add some to a bath; or place in a water-filled mister bottle to enhance your environment.

Centaury (*Centaurium umbellatum*)

Being of service is the raison d'être for Virgoans, a virtue that has become your calling card. With friends, family, and co-workers clamoring for your advice, assistance, and time, it's often challenging for a Virgoan to know when to say no. Centaury flower essence can help you draw boundaries, gracefully maintaining your giving nature and dedication to others without feeling enslaved by the needs of those around you. It can help you realize that saying no is sometimes as healing for you, and others, as saying yes.

Pine (*Pinus sylvestris*)

Virgoans hold everything—most notably themselves—to very high standards. Consequently, as a perfectionist, you may be haunted with self-reproach when a situation doesn't yield the outcome you intended. You may view this lack of success as a reflection of personal failure, even if it was a situation over which you really had little control. Pine is a great flower essence to help you release self-deprecating feelings and realize that the perfection you should strive for is complete and unconditional self-acceptance.

Rock Water

Efficient Virgoans like to organize themselves by way of schedules, routines, and systems, with order bringing them a sense of comfort. While this ritualized approach to life can make you more productive, it can also hamper your spontaneity, which is an important ingredient of joy and creativity. Rock Water flower essence allows you to engage the energy of the two elements represented in its name: the solidity of the rock combined with the fluid energy of water.

libra

SUN IN LIBRA ★ September 23–October 22

CHARACTERISTICS ★ Diplomatic / Poised / Equitable /
Judicious / Indecisive / Sociable / Stylish / Strong willed /
Charming / Orderly / Gracious / Frivolous

SYMBOL ★ The *Scales*, a symbol of justice, harmony, balance,
and equality. Reflective of Libra's association with measurement
and value, the "libra" was the basic unit of weight in ancient
Rome. In mythological and cultural traditions, the Scales are a
symbol of law, truth, morality, and the measurement of goodness
and purity.

PLANETARY RULER ★ *Venus*, known for being the brightest
planet in our solar system. Venus was the Roman goddess of
beauty and love, who represented sexuality, pleasure, and fertility. Her counterpart in Greek mythology was Aphrodite. In
astrology, Venus represents sensuality, harmony, and the force
of attraction.

ELEMENT ★ *Air*, characterized by the agile energy of thoughts,
observation, and logic. It is social, intellectual, changeable, and
relationship oriented.

QUALITY ★ *Cardinal*, which represents the initiation of the
creative cycle. It reflects ambition, enterprise, speed, and a self-
starting force that propels energy into the world.

Librans dislike when things are out of balance, including their health. Since you appreciate the beauty of harmony, any symptom of *dis*-ease—even one that would be perceived as inconsequential to most—registers strongly on the Libran's wellness scale.

When you do feel off-kilter, you'll work hard to find resolution to your problems and negotiate your way back to health. To do so, Librans often seek the advice of their large social networks—friends and acquaintances alike—to find the most respected health-care practitioner to help restore their physical equipoise. As you place a good deal of faith in the power of relationships, you're likely to find it more gratifying and effective to work with a health-care practitioner than travel the wellness path solo.

Yet, poised Librans are not quick to make decisions regarding their health care (or much else, for that matter). With the Scales as your astrological totem, a sharp-minded Libran will weigh all the pros and cons of various options—seeking second and sometimes third opinions whenever possible. While this judicious approach to decision making often results in very satisfying and beneficial outcomes, be careful that it doesn't lead to excessive procrastination, a Libran pitfall.

While those born under the sign of the Scales may seem outwardly calm and collected, Librans tends to carry around their fair share of stress, a result of the agitation they experience when faced with disagreeable situations. While disinclined to overtly express your woes (thinking it too brash for your refined Libran sensibilities), your disquietude may instead be expressed in your body, especially in the Libra-associated lower back, kidneys, and skin.

Librans will be more motivated to be active in their wellness journeys if they involve activities that are luxurious, pleasurable, and refined, characteristics that speak fluently to your sybaritic nature. For example, Librans will favor a weight loss diet that allows a daily dose of wine and chocolate over one that requires ascetic sacrifice. Reflecting your cooperative and social nature, finding a workout partner or inviting a friend to join you at the day spa will help you stay more interested and engaged in your personal wellness program.

 ## AREAS OF HEALTH FOCUS

Each zodiac sign is associated with certain parts of the body. These may be inherent areas of vulnerability, but when attended to, they can become areas of strength. The parts of the body associated with Libra include the following:

★ The **lumbar region**, the vertebrae in your lower back, which helps you to stand tall

★ The **islets of Langerhans**, a group of pancreatic cells that synthesize blood sugar–regulating insulin

★ The **kidneys**, the two bean-shaped organs balanced on either side of your spine, which are responsible for maintaining homeostasis

★ The **skin**, the organ that sheathes your body and serves as an interface with the environment

Your Libran resilient will, solution-seeking mind, and need for harmony are some of the resources you can use when facing any health challenge.

Back Up Back Health

In the name of peace and harmony, Librans tend to bend over backward for others. While your gracious and accommodating disposition is second nature, it isn't without its stress, which often takes refuge in the Libra-ruled lower back, translating into pain and stiffness. Chiropractic, massage, and acupuncture can be beneficial in promoting back health as can graceful, yet strengthening, fitness approaches such as Pilates and Gyrotonics. Ensuring your work space has good ergonomics and your mattress is adequately supportive can also be helpful whether you have a bad back or just want to prevent one. Also, when shopping for shoes, consider function as well as fashion; unsupportive shoes—including those stylish high heels that Librans love to wear—can throw your back out of whack.

Maintain Blood Sugar Balance

The innate Libran temperament is one of equilibrium. Yet with your sign's planetary ruler, Venus, associated with both blood sugar and the insulin-producing islets of Langerhans, balance may not come as naturally to your glucose levels. While there can be a genetic component to developing blood sugar imbalances, lifestyle factors are just as—if not more—important, making this area of your health one in which you can exert a good level of control. Maintaining optimal weight and switching to a whole foods diet can keep blood sugar in check. A regular fitness routine is beneficial, too, as exercise improves your cells' sensitivity to insulin, which helps maintain glucose balance.

Support Your Kidneys

In pure Libran fashion, the role of the kidneys—ruled by your sign in medical astrology—is focused on maintaining homeostasis. The kidneys keep balance by ridding the body of waste, excess water, and surplus electrolytes. Diabetes and hypertension can impinge on kidney health, as can smoking. Drinking six to eight glasses of water each day is important for keeping the kidneys—and the rest of the body—in tip-top shape. In traditional Chinese medicine, it is said that the kidneys are negatively affected by fear; therefore, working on feeling more empowered may do wonders for the health of these organs, let alone your general well-being.

Enhance Skin Health

Librans love all things refined, including physical beauty, which is one reason they pay close attention to, and take pride in, their appearance. So the fact that natives of your sign are prone to skin issues—including breakouts and dermatitis—may seem like a cruel irony. You can do many things to promote skin health and put your "best face" forward: watch that Libran tendency to over-indulge in sweets and alcohol; help your kidneys flush out toxins by keeping yourself well hydrated; and take the time to follow a thorough skin-care regimen, including regular cleansing, exfoliating, moisturizing, and sun protection.

 HEALTHY EATING TIPS

Being sociable, Librans enjoy numerous opportunities to enjoy delicious meals in the company of others. While this can bring you pleasure, it can also pose a challenge to sticking to a healthy-eating plan.

Eat for Blood Sugar Balance

If you would like to keep your blood sugar balanced, consider some simple dietary strategies. Eat whole foods, such as vegetables, fruits, beans, and whole grains, which are rich in fiber and anti-oxidants. Also, cut down on refined sugars, processed carbohydrates, and animal protein, excesses of which can increase diabetes risk. Eating several small meals throughout the day, rather than larger ones spaced far apart, can help keep glucose levels poised.

★ You can further refine a blood sugar–balancing diet by favoring foods with a low glycemic index (GI). Low-GI foods are those that break down slowly and don't cause rapid elevations of blood sugar. Detailed information about the glycemic index can be found in numerous books and websites.

Infuse Meals with Graciousness

The artistic Libran has an inherent need for aesthetic fulfillment, and beauty around you nurtures a sense of peace within. Take this into consideration when preparing meals by turning them into small works of art. This will enhance your enjoyment of food and make meals even more soulfully nourishing.

★ Make each dining experience one of artistic beauty. Pretty plates and serving pieces can add grandeur to even the simplest of meals. Use candles, place mats, and cloth napkins to further enhance the elegance of your meal (regardless of whether it's a four-course feast with friends, or take-out Thai on your own).

Trust Your Gut

Librans have a propensity for indecision that can extend to their ability to make food choices. Even the smallest of considerations can seem monumental at the time. This is especially true when you're in the company of others, compounding your dilemma; after all, you care what people think of you and don't want to make the "wrong choice."

★ Tune into your inner voice at mealtimes; it knows what is best in the moment. Remember, though, that oftentimes there is no one best option, but equally good choices. You can make a decision today, safe in the knowledge that tomorrow will provide an opportunity for another experience.

 # HEALTH-SUPPORTING FOODS

As Librans always want to strike a balance, it's nice to know that there are many foods that can provide you with both pleasure *and* health-promoting benefits. Foods associated with your planetary ruler, Venus, that support Libran health include berries, beans, and artichokes.

Berries

Brimming with nutrients, especially phytonutrients with anticancer and anti-inflammatory properties, Venus-ruled berries can spruce up your health. Raspberries and blackberries are especially rich in fiber, while cranberries may help prevent kidney stones. Berries are considered a low to medium glycemic index food and therefore won't elevate blood sugar as much as many other fruits.

★ Enjoy berries in smoothies, salads, and a range of delicious desserts, from cobblers to fruit salads. If fresh berries aren't readily accessible, buy packaged frozen ones. Luckily, freezing is a great way to preserve the nutrients in fruits.

Beans

Looking to keep your blood sugar on an even keel? Enjoy more beans. High in fiber and protein, and low on the glycemic index, these little treasures help balance glucose levels and may reduce the risk of developing diabetes. Whether they are black, kidney, navy, or garbanzo, you can't make a wrong decision when adding beans to your meal plan.

★ To reduce their cooking time and enhance their digestibility, presoak your beans. Place them in a bowl, cover them with water, and keep the bowl in the refrigerator for at least eight hours. To cook them, use two parts fresh water to one part beans, and simmer for about an hour and fifteen minutes.

Artichokes

It's no surprise that artichokes are another Venus-ruled food. After all, even the process of eating one is sensual, as are the taste and texture of its delicate heart. This fact wasn't lost on the ancient Romans, who held artichokes in high esteem as aphrodisiacs. Yet these Venusian properties aren't all they provide—artichokes help you finely tune your health by offering good amounts of fiber, folic acid, and potassium.

★ Artichokes are surprisingly simple to prepare. Cut off the bottom stem so the artichokes are balanced while cooking. Remove the first few outer leaves, and trim one-half inch off the top. Place in a steamer bowl, and cook until the outer leaves readily pull away from the center, about twenty to forty minutes, depending upon size.

SPA AND WELLNESS THERAPIES

With the goddess of beauty ruling your sign, pampering treatments that help you look your best hold great value to a Libran's sense of wellness.

Sugar Body Polish

A sugar body polish is a great spa treatment for Librans who like everything, including their skin, to be smooth and refined. Not only does sugar's granular texture help slough off dead skin cells, but sugar also contains glycolic acid, which further adds to its exfoliation properties. Polished skin not only looks better but it also translates into better health as this process encourages the skin to breathe and shed impurities.

★ Look for treatments that use evaporated sugarcane juice rather than refined sugar, as the former offers many more benefits. Sugar body polish treatments often contain other ingredients—such as fruit and botanical extracts—added for their therapeutic and cosmetic properties.

Lomilomi Massage

To a Libran, relationships are works of art; like any masterpiece, they are deeply inspiring, satisfying, and healing. Lomilomi, a traditional Hawaiian massage practice, offers a Libran another way to benefit from relationships as this massage is often performed by not one but two practitioners. Working in unison, they rhythmically massage different parts of your body. In addition to relieving muscular tension, lomilomi does wonders for relieving mental tension.

★ A lomilomi massage performed by a sole practitioner can also provide you with many benefits. That's because this massage style, often referred to as "loving hands," calls on gracefulness, dance-inspired movements, and intuition, qualities a Libran greatly appreciates.

Facials

Even if beauty is only skin-deep, it's still important to take care of your skin. Facials can do wonders for making your skin glow and helping you to feel beautiful inside and out. During a facial your skin is exfoliated, deeply cleansed, and moisturized. You're also treated to a face and scalp massage that is not only sumptuous but also therapeutic, as it stimulates the lymphatic system to clear away impurities that may contribute to a less-than-radiant appearance.

★ Spas usually offer basic facials as well as ones that feature additional techniques, including oxygen treatments, dermabrasion procedures, or glycolic peels. Aestheticians can customize a facial to your particular skin type and concerns.

RELAXATION PRACTICES

Librans are most peaceful when beauty and accord surround them and when they feel free to express the inherent grace and artistry they naturally embrace.

Feng Shui

As Librans are so sensitive to disharmony, if your environment isn't in order, it can make you feel "out of order." To enjoy a deeper sense of harmony, consider feng shui-ing your living and/or work space. Feng shui—known as the Chinese art of placement—uses furniture positioning, color choice, and auspicious items (such as wind chimes) to unblock energetic disturbances in the environment that are thought to inhibit one's ability to acquire good fortune and achieve optimal health.

★ Feng shui has become more popular in the West, making it easy to find books and websites on the subject. If you don't want to learn the techniques yourself, you can always hire a trained practitioner to feng shui your space.

Tai Chi

Grace in action could as easily describe a Libran as it could tai chi. This martial arts form has gained popularity in the West as a serene approach to exercise and stress relief. Tai chi features slow dancelike movements, with each pose flowing seamlessly into the next. It's a moving meditation that provides the body with an opportunity to gain agility and strength.

★ Although there are many books and videos on tai chi available, learning from a qualified instructor in a class setting can provide you with the personalized, yet social, experience that Librans appreciate. Look for tai chi classes at community centers, health clubs, and colleges in your area.

Writing Poetry

Librans are so concerned that their words or actions will cause discord that they often restrain their true self-expression. Therefore, it can be especially important to find supportive outlets, such as writing poetry, that give you freedom to openly articulate your creative mind. Aligned with your innate sense of grace, poetry honors words not only for their ability to express meaning but also for the aesthetic qualities they embody.

★ Writing haikus, in particular, may be a good poetry practice for a Libran. These short poetic verses, composed of just three lines and seventeen syllables, can provide you with an opportunity to balance the desire for expressing meaning with the need to maintain a well-defined order.

YOGA POSES

Yoga can help Librans foster strength and flexibility in their bodies and equanimity in their minds.

Tree Pose (*Vrksasana*)

Tree Pose—one of the basic balance postures in yoga—can help reinforce a Libran's sense of equilibrium. The key to balancing, as every Libran may know, is to be strong yet supple—just like a tree.

★ Stand tall with your feet together. After shifting your weight to your right foot, lift your left leg, and grab your ankle with your left hand. Place the sole of your left foot on your inner right thigh or calf. Bring your palms together in front of your heart, lightly gazing at a spot several feet in front of you to help you balance. Stay in the posture for up to one minute. Return to the original standing pose, and repeat on the other side.

Lord of the Dance Pose (*Natarajasana*)

This elegant asana allows Librans to express their gracefulness. In addition to inspiring balance, this standing posture helps to tone the lumbar muscles, lengthen the lower spine, and stimulate the kidneys.

★ Stand tall with your feet together. After shifting your weight to your right foot, lift your left leg behind you, bending your knee so that your foot is reaching toward your buttocks. Grab your left foot with your left hand. Pushing your left foot into your hand will help you work toward bringing your left thigh parallel to the floor. As you do this, stretch your right arm in front of you, parallel to the floor, and gently lean forward. Stay in the pose for up to thirty seconds, and repeat on the other side.

Boat Pose (*Navasana*)

Boat Pose provides an alternative way—a seated posture—in which to practice balance. This posture strengthens the lower back and energizes the kidneys.

★ Sit on the floor with your knees bent and your feet on the floor. Hold the back of your lower thighs with your hands. Your sternum should be lifted and your torso slightly leaning back. Rock back so that your feet come off the floor and you're balancing on your sit bones. Have your shins parallel to the floor, or if possible, try to straighten your legs. Remove your hands, straightening your arms so that they point toward your feet and are parallel to the floor. Stay in the pose for one minute.

 AROMATHERAPY

Aromatherapy offers a Libran an exquisitely delightful way to experience wellness. Fragrant essential oils not only smell wonderful but you can also use them cosmetically in creams and toners to enhance your beauty.

Damask Rose (*Rosa damascena*)

If one flower is associated with the Venusian concepts of beauty and love, it's the rose. In addition to featuring a heart-opening fragrance, oil made from the damask rose has radiant skin-enhancing properties. While a Libran may like the equanimity of the fair-minded sentiment "A rose is a rose is a rose," it doesn't actually hold true for different types of damask rose oils: rose otto is preferable over rose absolute as the former is not extracted using chemical solvents.

★ Damask rose makes a gorgeous perfume. Add it to your bathwater for a luxuriously romantic experience. As rose oil is very expensive (it takes thousands of pounds of rose petals to make one ounce of oil), it is often diluted with jojoba oil.

Rose Geranium (*Pelargonium graveolens*)

A cousin of the red-colored geraniums that adorn many window-sills, rose geranium is one of the premier skin-care oils. Like a Libran, it doesn't discriminate—it can create balance in either overly dry or oily skin. It is also an energizing pick-me-up, inspiring the mind and body when stress or fatigue drains your energy reserves. The scent of rose geranium is said to inspire relaxed spontaneity, helpful to Librans when they feel encumbered by indecision.

★ For a skin-balancing toner, add some rose geranium oil to a mister bottle of water, or mix some oil into your favorite cleansing mask. With its warm and rosy scent, it also makes a lovely perfume.

Peppermint (*Mentha piperita*)

A symbol of hospitality in many cultures, Venus-ruled peppermint is conducive to good health, including many Libran wellness concerns. When your solution-searching mind needs a bit of a boost, you'll appreciate mint's ability to relieve mental fatigue and enhance concentration. It also has renowned stomach-soothing properties, making it a wonderful digestive aid, especially after a rich and heavy meal.

★ Add some peppermint oil to your facial cleanser to help balance out any red or dry patches. The smell of mint is a refreshing way to start your day, giving your brain an early morning boost. For a delicious after-meal stomach settler, enjoy a cup of mint tea.

NATURAL REMEDIES

Herbs, dietary supplements, and other natural remedies can do justice to a self-care regimen aimed at promoting optimal health.

Fenugreek (*Trigonella foenum-graecum*)

Librans can benefit from fenugreek's beautifying properties. Mix ground seeds with water for calming skin irritations, or with some yogurt as a traditional Indian hair conditioner. One of fenugreek's traditional uses, helping those with diabetes, has been supported by studies that show that it lowers blood sugar and total cholesterol levels. Traditional Chinese medicine also uses it for kidney ailments.

★ Fenugreek is available as a supplement in capsule or liquid tincture form. You can find fenugreek seeds, which you can grind at home and use in recipes (it is actually a staple of curry blends), in the spice section of natural food stores and specialty food markets.

Burdock (*Arctium lappa*)

Although it may not be the most elegant plant, that doesn't stop burdock from being governed by your planetary ruler, Venus. After all, with its clinging burs, it is tenacious, just like the mythic goddess herself. With its numerous benefits, it can clear up many health imbalances. Burdock is known as a blood purifier, diuretic, and promoter of kidney health. This is likely why it has traditionally been used to help control breakouts and bolster the appearance of the skin.

★ Burdock root is available in capsule or liquid tincture form. Fresh burdock root, found at Asian food markets, is also a commonly consumed therapeutic food in Japanese cuisine.

Evening Primrose Oil (*Oenothera biennis*)

Imbalances—notably those occurring in levels of fatty acids, such as gamma-linolenic acid (GLA)—can lead to a host of different conditions, many associated with Libran health. For example, those who experience PMS, dermatitis, and diabetes are thought to have a compromised ability to synthesize GLA. Adding a concentrated source of this fatty acid to the diet—such as in the form of evening primrose oil supplements—has been found to relieve the symptoms of these conditions and to promote hair and nail health.

★ Evening primrose oil is generally available in soft capsules. To enhance absorption, take with meals. Buy evening primrose oil from a high-quality manufacturer to avoid purchasing a product adulterated with less expensive safflower or soybean oil.

FLOWER ESSENCES

That these healing elixirs are made from beautiful flowers is one reason that Librans will be attracted to flower essences. All flower essences can be used similarly: mix a few drops in a glass of water, and drink several times a day; add some to a bath; or place in a water-filled mister bottle to enhance your environment.

Scleranthus (*Scleranthus annuus*)

As the diplomats of the zodiac, Librans possess a deep-seated desire for mediating resolution. Yet, while you are masterful at helping others make decisions, it is somewhat more challenging for Librans to do so in their own personal lives, owing to the fear that they'll choose wrongly or alienate others. When you need help connecting with your innate wisdom to make a choice most aligned with your personal needs and values, try Scleranthus flower essence.

Scarlet Monkeyflower (*Mimulus cardinalis*)

While Librans appear easygoing, with your heightened sensitivity to injustice, your internal sense of peace may often be ruffled, eliciting discord or even anger within. Yet harmony-loving Librans are more inclined to repress these "ugly" emotions than outwardly express them. While you are no doubt known for grace under pressure, continually suppressing negative feelings can contribute to a sense of discord and even out-of-character outbursts. Scarlet Monkeyflower can help you honestly connect with and express your full range of feelings so you can maintain emotional poise.

Pretty Face (*Triteleia ixioides*)

Librans like to look their best as it helps them to feel their best. Yet focusing too much on your physical appearance can be stressful, draining your energy, time, and even cash flow. Pretty Face flower essence can help break the pattern of being overly identified with one's external image, helping you to see that you are more than just a pretty face and that your true source of beauty lies deep within.

scorpio

SUN IN SCORPIO ★ October 23–November 21

CHARACTERISTICS ★ Passionate / Forceful / Intense / Determined / Brooding / Resilient / Probing / Regenerative / Emotional / Combative / Resourceful / Secretive

SYMBOL ★ The *Scorpion*, an animal known for thriving in the dark, stealthily moving in shadow, and protecting itself with its venomous sting. In mythological and cultural traditions, the Scorpion is the guardian of the entrance to the underworld and a symbol of protection and retribution.

PLANETARY RULER ★ *Pluto*, now considered a dwarf planet, travels both above and below the orbital plane of the solar system. Pluto was the Roman god of the underworld (governing over the dead) and society's wealth (ruling over the mined riches of the world). His counterpart in Greek mythology was Hades. In astrology, Pluto represents survival instincts, extreme power, and the death and rebirth cycle of transformation.

ELEMENT ★ *Water*, characterized by the fluid energy of emotion, reflection, and nonlinear understanding. It is sensitive, personal, and responsive.

QUALITY ★ *Fixed*, which represents the planning and building phase of the creative cycle. It reflects reliability, predictability, and a disciplined force that persists in creating structure.

Scorpios have incredible regenerative abilities that can serve as powerful allies in their personal health care. You have a cogent capacity to heal yourself, aided by a deep-seated awareness that your mind and emotions play an inextricable role in your physical well-being.

When Scorpios don't feel up to par, they don't just settle into passivity or even self-pity. After all, Scorpios are charter members of Nietzsche's "What doesn't kill us makes us stronger" club. You'll dive right in with deep resolve to counter any challenges you may face. And since Scorpios are the detectives of the zodiac, you'll passionately commit to finding the cause of and solution to any malady, leaving no stone unturned as you search for answers in places that others may never even consider looking.

When it comes to a wellness routine, Scorpios would much rather work hard, marshalling their formidable inner strength, than be passive or pampered. You like transformative experiences in which you can come up against—and subsequently raze—your perceived limitations, allowing you to plunge more deeply into the substratum of your personal power. Therefore, to rid yourself of impurities and regenerate your body and mind, you're likely to be attracted to the intensity provided by boot camp workouts, detox diets, deep-tissue massages, and other activities that challenge your will and resilience.

Maintaining control and personal power is a central theme in a Scorpio's life. If you feel under the weather, you probably keep it to yourself. You may reason that you don't need others' help, plus you're not inclined to risk having someone perceive you as weak. After all, Scorpios want to be in charge of their destinies and don't want to give any other impression.

Consequently, you may be less inclined than others to seek out the advice of a physician, not trusting that someone else—even a supposed authority—can readily help you find solutions specific to your personal needs. Of course, sometimes even resourceful Scorpios would do well to garner the advice and aid of others, notably those well trained in their area of expertise.

AREAS OF HEALTH FOCUS

Each zodiac sign is associated with certain parts of the body. These may be inherent areas of vulnerability, but when attended to, they can become areas of strength. The parts of the body associated with Scorpio include the following:

★ The **pelvic region**, **genitals**, and **reproductive organs**, which allow you to experience pleasure and create life

★ The **urinary tract** and **bladder**, which excrete filtered metabolic waste products

★ The **large intestine**, which hosts the last stage of digestion and the processing of undigested food for final passage out of the body

Your Scorpionic deep resolve, powerful regenerative capacity, and ability to dig deep to find solutions are some of the resources you can use when facing any health challenge.

Embrace All Stages of Life

The transformative ability to create new life—and the reproductive organs associated with that facility—fall under the domain of Scorpio. Consequently, in medical astrology, both menses and menopause are associated with your sign. Female Scorpios are obviously not the only ones to experience these biological events. But, as one whose nature thrives on metamorphosis, a Scorpio may experience these life processes on a more deeply psychological level than others. While whole foods, natural remedies, and yoga can help smooth out the hormonal roller coaster that both menses and menopause bring, embracing each stage of your womanhood as it unfolds can be deeply healing as well.

Protect Against UTIs

While Scorpios may crave intensity, even they don't like the kind of intense symptoms that accompany an infection of the urinary tract, a part of the body ruled by your sign. You can reduce your chances of getting a urinary tract infection (UTI) by doing some simple things: drink lots of water, wear breathable cotton underwear, and empty your bladder before and after having intercourse. If you do get an infection and have to use antibiotics, consider taking probiotics as well. These supplements will help safeguard your beneficial intestinal flora from those antibacterial medications.

Maintain Regularity

While a complex Scorpio might not consider herself to be "regular," when it comes to your health, being regular is important, especially since your sign rules the large intestine. Bowel irregularity, often experienced as bouts of constipation, can reduce energy, impede weight loss, and detract from a sense of vitality. A fiber-rich diet can help keep things moving smoothly and promote optimal intestinal health. Activities that reduce stress—including exercise, yoga, and meditation—are also beneficial for the resilient Scorpio's digestive health.

Curb Habits That Undermine Health

Scorpios tend to submerge themselves in a sea of feelings. While this stygian journey into your emotional recesses speaks to your sign's inherent need for plumbing the depths, if you don't come up to the surface every now and then, it can leave you feeling overwhelmed. Looking for a way to cope with the intensity, Scorpios often turn to a bottle of wine, a pack of cigarettes, another cup of coffee, or some other drug of choice. While going to the dark is part of your nature, take a flashlight with you—in the form of support from your friends or family, a therapist, or a detached attitude. That way you are more likely to avoid behaviors that can put your health at risk.

 HEALTHY EATING TIPS

Eating is a deeply transformative Scorpionic experience; after all, the foods you consume get broken down so your body can rebuild and remake itself. That's why nutrient-rich whole foods are so important, as they provide your body with the resources it needs for optimal replenishment.

Don't Rely on Food for Solace

Scorpios are passionate creatures. The feelings you experience can seem so deep and all-consuming that you probably imagine that no one, save a fellow Scorpio, can comprehend them. Therefore, if solace can't be found in a relationship, you will seek it elsewhere, which is where emotional eating can come into play. Unfortunately, eating as a refuge from intense emotions doesn't solve any problems—it just creates new ones.

★ Before seeking consolation in a box of cookies, stop and ask yourself what else you can do to feel supported instead. If you find it hard to put a stop to emotional eating, keep carrots, celery, or jicama on hand. Munching on them can provide the cathartic release you seek without the caloric baggage.

Practice Moderation

Scorpios have a tendency to go to extremes. Whatever you do, you commit to and do with full force, diving deep into the experience, which provides you with the emotional charge you crave. Yet if you go to extremes with your eating habits—for example, binge-ing and/or being overly restrictive with your food intake—it can have less-than-supportive effects on your health.

★ Not only can extreme eating behaviors lead to unhealthy weight gain or loss, but they can also affect your nerves, metabolism, and mental outlook. Exploring your relationship with food under the guidance of a skilled nutritionist may provide you with deep insights into yourself, something that Scorpios crave.

Try a Detox Diet

Like the mythic phoenix, a Scorpio understands that new life can emerge only after the old one is relinquished. Following a detox diet can help you experience this deep regeneration on a physical level as it allows your body to eliminate compounds that may tax your vitality. And since Scorpios like to challenge their will, and limiting food intake is nothing if not challenging, you're likely to find this process engaging as well.

★ Detox diets can range from a one-day fast to several weeks of avoid-ing all suspected food allergens; tune into your body to find the approach that feels best for you. Take note, though: with a tendency to go to extremes, it's important for Scorpios to view a detox diet as a periodic healing ritual rather than an ongoing dietary approach.

 HEALTH-SUPPORTING FOODS

Scorpios may be drawn to foods that are deeply colored and intense in flavor. Beneficial foods include dark chocolate, cranberries, and fermented foods such as yogurt, kefir, kimchi, and sauerkraut.

Dark Chocolate

Scorpios' love of the dark can come in handy when choosing chocolate with the most health benefits. Darker chocolates have a higher content of cacao and therefore a greater amount of heart-healthy flavonoid antioxidants. Chocolate's allure also extends to its reputation as an aphrodisiac, a boon for sensually oriented Scorpios.

★ Grate some chocolate onto a fruit salad; berries and chocolate are a particularly delicious pairing. Mix cocoa powder and honey into plain yogurt for a healthy dessert. While chocolate may have benefits, it's not, unfortunately, a cure-all. So curb a Scorpionic tendency to over-indulge, and instead enjoy this treat in moderation.

Cranberries

Cranberries, like Scorpios, are known for their sharp bite and powerful healing abilities. Once thought of solely as Thanksgiving fare, cranberries now appear in dishes throughout the year. Their growing popularity is related to research that shows this little antioxidant-rich fruit to be a potent weapon against developing infections of the Scorpio-ruled urinary tract.

★ To avoid empty calories, purchase cranberry juice concentrate—which you can reconstitute with water and a little natural sweetener—instead of presweetened cranberry juice cocktail. It's easy to make your own cranberry sauce: just simmer fresh or frozen berries in honey-sweetened orange juice for about fifteen minutes, until they split or pop open.

Fermented Foods

Scorpios are masters of change; as you transform and evolve, you become more connected to your inherent power. The same can be said for fermented foods—such as yogurt, kefir, kimchi, and sauerkraut. For example, when bacterial cultures are added to milk, breaking down its lactose sugars, the result is foods that are easier to digest, such as yogurt and kefir. Additionally, the beneficial bacteria added to ferment foods repopulates our own supply of health-giving intestinal flora, a key to optimal well-being.

★ Look for high-quality yogurts that include an array of live active bacterial cultures, ideally more than just the *L. bulgaricus* and *S. thermophilus* bacteria that are typically added. Kefir is a delicious drinkable alternative to yogurt. Sauerkraut and kimchi, the spicy Korean side dish, are flavorful accompaniments to a variety of dishes.

SPA AND WELLNESS THERAPIES

If you set your mind to transformation, you'll do whatever it takes—including signing up for a host of spa and wellness therapies—to achieve it.

Rolfing

Rolfing is a form of bodywork that targets the soft tissue web known as *fascia*, the covering that envelops muscles, nerves, and bones. Releasing bound and tight fascia is thought to transform deep-seated patterns of misalignment, leading to reduced chronic pain, freer motion, and greater structural integration. Like a Scorpio, Rolfing goes deep, so you may experience slight discomfort during a session. Though, if any sign is able to handle a bit of temporary pain for long-lasting gain, it's a Scorpio.

★ As Rolfing is organized into ten sessions, it requires a commitment. Yet Scorpios are nothing if not committed, adhering loyally to those things in which they believe. To find a certified Rolfing practitioner, go to www.rolf.org.

Mud Treatments

Scorpios like exploring a full range of experiences and don't mind getting their hands a little dirty, both figuratively and literally, in the process. So why not get your whole body dirty to clean up your health by enjoying a mud treatment? Being mired in mineral-rich mud, whether as a body mask or in a bath filled with this enriching earthy material, can help relax muscles, improve circulation, and aid in detoxification.

★ Mud treatments are also known as *fangotherapy* or *pelotherapy*. You can also enjoy their benefits at home by purchasing mud and applying it to your knees, legs, or other sore areas.

Colonics

As a Scorpio, you don't shy away from things, even those that other people find unseemly and crude, if you believe that there is some merit in experiencing them. Therefore, you're more likely than natives of other signs not only to schedule a colonic but also to really appreciate the benefits that this treatment can offer. By infusing water into the Scorpio-ruled large intestine, colonics help to flush out excess waste materials from the body. Proponents note that this aids in both detoxification and better digestion.

★ Make sure to find a colon hydrotherapist who is licensed and uses disposable and sterile equipment. Ask the therapist to recommend foods or supplements that can help replenish any good intestinal bacteria that may get washed away during a treatment.

RELAXATION PRACTICES

Scorpios can relax the most when they feel safe expressing their uniquely deep natures, which like to discover hidden truths.

Neo-Tantra

Scorpios have an affinity for provocative experiences that allow them to transcend their egos, enabling their deeper selves to emerge. As such, you may gain great benefit from practicing neo-tantra, a modern-day translation of the Buddhist and Hindu disciplines that honor sex as a vehicle for spiritual elevation. Neo-tantric rituals focus on stimulating chakra energy centers, honoring the deep essence of your partner, and experiencing sex as a consciousness-elevating experience.

★ There are many books available on neo-tantra and sacred sexuality. Neo-tantra workshops are also available; as these courses offer varying degrees of exploration, make sure you thoroughly research the teacher and how the course is organized before signing up.

Kundalini Yoga

The sign of Scorpio is associated with a very deep transformational power. In mystic traditions, the root of this power is known as *prana* (the Sanskrit word for life force), much of it being concentrated at the base of the spine, where it is called *kundalini*. One method for accessing this power and the vitality it yields is the practice of kundalini yoga, an energy-focused style of yoga distinct from those practiced at most studios.

★ Inquire at your local yoga studio to see if they offer classes in this type of yoga. As kundalini is very physically and energetically intense, it's advisable to have guidance when working with it rather than doing so on your own.

Mysteries

Adept at clueing into others' hidden motives and equipped with a keen interest in leaving no stone unturned, a Scorpio loves a good mystery. Indulging your inner Miss Marple by burying yourself in a detective novel is a great way for a Scorpio to unwind. If you want a more lifelike whodunit experience, consider attending a mystery theatre performance or participating in a murder mystery getaway retreat.

★ Doing an Internet search will readily turn up many different murder mystery retreats available throughout the country. If you'd rather play Sherlock Holmes at home, buy a whodunit game kit, and invite some friends over for a deadly good time.

YOGA POSES

Because Scorpio is a fixed sign, the practice of yoga is beneficial for you as it can inspire flexibility in both body and mind.

Garland Pose (*Malasana*)

Intense like a Scorpio, this wide squat pose is sure to unfasten any tightness in your pelvis, stretching your groin and bringing energy to your genital region. It also benefits the urinary tract, and, as you'll notice, is an amazing hip opener.

★ With your feet close together, move into a squat, separating your knees so they are slightly wider than your torso. Reach your torso forward with your arms outstretched. Then swing your arms around the outside of your legs, reaching for the backs of your ankles with your hands. Hold this position for up to one minute.

Wide-Angle Seated Forward Bend (*Upavistha Konasana*)

While Scorpios aren't known for compromise, you may like this seemingly compromising position, as it can be a great teacher. It allows you to see how you respond when you meet your limits, fostering an ability to accept your boundaries with emotional honesty.

★ Sit on the floor with your legs straight in front of you and your spine elongated. Open your legs out to the side as far as feels comfortable.

Make sure both your knees and toes point upward. With a lengthened torso, lean forward and place your hands on the ground, finding a position that is challenging but not painful. Stay in the pose for up to two minutes.

Dead Bug Pose (*Ananda Balasana*)

It takes a special breed—notably a Scorpio who is fascinated by the darker things in life—to appreciate a posture called Dead Bug Pose. This asana is at once gently restorative (allowing you to maintain a sense of control) and intensely provocative (as your groin and leg muscles succumb to a state of relaxation).

★ Lie on your back with your knees bent and your feet touching the floor. Slowly bend your knees into your torso, and grab the outsides of your feet. Ideally, your feet should be above your knees with your shins perpendicular to the floor. Gently pull your feet toward your hips so that your knees come closer to your torso. Keep your lower back lengthened and pressed down toward the ground. Stay in the pose for up to one minute.

 AROMATHERAPY

Aromatherapy is a deeply alchemical process, something that transformation-inclined Scorpios will appreciate.

Ylang-Ylang (*Cananga odorata*)

Sex can be very powerful for a Scorpio. Yet, if you deny your innate sensual nature, libidinal lethargy can set in. If your hots are a little cool, try ylang-ylang, one of the most well-known aphrodisiac scents. You needn't scatter ylang-ylang flowers on your bed as some newly married couples in Indonesia do—just add the flower's essential oil to your personal care repertoire.

★ Wear ylang-ylang as a perfume. For a twist on the traditional Indonesian marriage bed, spritz your linens with an ylang-ylang and water mixture. Add a few drops of ylang-ylang to coconut oil, and apply as a South Pacific–inspired hair treatment.

Basil (*Ocimum basilicum*)

According to superstition, basil leaves could transform themselves into your astrological totem, the Scorpion. While this may be folkloric fancy, basil essential oil can certainly transform your health. It is said to help integrate the conscious and subconscious minds, promoting psychic vision. Basil is noted for its emmenagogue properties, useful for stimulating and normalizing menstrual flow.

★ Rub some basil-infused massage oil on your tummy during that time of the month. As basil can also act as an insect repellent, applying body lotion mixed with a few drops of the essential oil may help keep vexing critters away.

Helichrysum (*Helichrysum italicum*)

Like your sign, helichrysum—also known as *everlasting*—is prized for its regenerative abilities. As such, it is one of the best oils to use for healing scars and wounds. When it comes to healing emotional scarring and wounds, the scent of helichrysum is also well suited. It helps to unblock deep subconscious emotions and stimulates a profound level of self-compassion, something with which a Scorpio may need assistance at times.

★ To help untangle knotted emotional energy, use helichrysum in a room diffuser to enjoy an uplifting environment. Add a few drops to massage oil for relief of aches and pain or to some moisturizer to bolster skin health.

NATURAL REMEDIES

When it comes to your health-care practitioners, watch a tendency to be secretive: tell them which natural remedies you use to be assured that none will negatively interact with any medications you may take.

Aloe Vera (*Aloe vera*)

Scorpio is a sign of timeless endurance; similarly, aloe vera was traditionally viewed as a symbol of eternal life. Aloe's regenerative properties provide great benefits when applied topically, helping to soften skin, heal cuts, and temper burns. Aloe vera juice is also one of the premier natural laxatives, a helpful remedy when the Scorpio-ruled intestine needs a little extra support.

★ Look for juice products that contain at least 99 percent aloe vera. For back-to-the-earth healing, buy an aloe plant; set it on a sunny sill, breaking open a leaf and extracting the gel when your skin needs some soothing.

Flaxseed (*Linum usitatissimum*)

Flaxseed is an incredibly rich source of fiber, helping to promote the health of the Scorpio-ruled large intestine as well as lower cholesterol levels. It also contains lignan phytonutrients, acclaimed for balancing hormone levels and reducing breast cancer risk. Additionally, flaxseed contains a large concentration of anti-inflammatory omega-3 fatty acids.

★ While flaxseed is thought of as a supplement, it can also be enjoyed as a food incorporated into your daily diet. For better absorption—and therefore greater benefits—it's important to use ground, rather than whole, flaxseed.

Black Cohosh (*Actaea racemosa*)

Black cohosh may be of benefit for Scorpios with painful periods or premenstrual syndrome. In several studies, it has also been found to provide relief from menopausal symptoms, such as hot flashes, insomnia, and anxiety. These female health benefits are not just recent discoveries, however. For centuries, the Native Americans used this "women's remedy herb" for a variety of gynecological challenges.

★ Researchers have yet to conclude whether black cohosh exerts its action through an estrogenlike activity or through an alternative mechanism. Therefore, if you take estrogenic medications or have concerns about your estrogen levels, consult a physician before using black cohosh. Herbalists recommend not taking this herb for more than six months at a time, owing to its powerful effects.

FLOWER ESSENCES

Flower essences evoke deep changes in one's psychological and emotional well-being, great for Scorpios looking for ways to be more aligned with their truly powerful natures. All flower essences can be used similarly: mix a few drops in a glass of water, and drink several times a day; add some to a bath; or place in a water-filled mister bottle to enhance your environment.

Mustard (*Sinapsis arvensis*)

Scorpios have a closer relationship with the subconscious than most. While this gives you the ability to experience an expansive range of powerful feelings, it can also engender a sense of gloom that seems to come out of nowhere. Understanding the reasons for your feelings can deepen your self-awareness and also reduce the potential for being blindsided by these seemingly out-of-the-blue mood swings. This is the realm of Mustard flower essence, which can help you plumb the emotional heaviness to shed light on the cause of the darkness that may reside within.

Basil (*Ocimum basilicum*)

As the Scorpionic nature has a great affinity for the powerful and the intense, sex can be a great avenue for experiencing profound emotions and interpersonal connection. It can also help you get in touch with your deep creative energies. However, if you feel shame concerning your sexuality (whether from past trauma or societal pressures), you may employ sensuality in ways that are not truly aligned with your emotions and desires. If you feel that your sex life is polarized from your heart's intentions, try Basil flower essence, which can help you reclaim and reintegrate this dynamic and joyfully creative part of yourself.

Holly (*Ilex aquifolium*)

Suspicious Scorpios don't often share the full range of their feelings with others (after all, you reason, "who would understand?"). Accordingly, you may believe that others aren't candid with you either. If your distrust paves the way toward isolation and anger, Holly flower essence may be a great remedy for you. It can help open your heart to the possibility that even if others have feelings and motives that they don't share with you, their intentions may come from a benevolent place, just as yours do.

sagittarius

SUN IN SAGITTARIUS ★ November 22–December 21

CHARACTERISTICS ★ Adventurous / Optimistic / Versatile / Zealous / Moral / Wise / Exuberant / Jovial / Capricious / Dogmatic / Philosophical / Inspired

SYMBOL ★ The *Archer* in the act of shooting an arrow, signifying the unbridled freedom of movement and a destination-oriented journey. It is pictured as a centaur, a mythic half-horse/half-human creature that represents the melding of our animal and spiritual natures. In mythological and cultural traditions, the centaur is a symbol of adventure, revelry, wisdom, and courage.

PLANETARY RULER ★ *Jupiter*, the largest planet in our solar system. Jupiter was the Roman king of the gods, who governed the universe and oversaw the laws of justice. His counterpart in Greek mythology was Zeus. In astrology, Jupiter represents understanding, expansion, integration, luck, and faith.

ELEMENT ★ *Fire*, characterized by the dynamic energy of inspiration, enthusiasm, and passion. It is transformative, kinetic, and action oriented.

QUALITY ★ *Mutable*, which represents the adjustment and finessing stage of the creative cycle. It reflects flexibility, tolerance, and an adaptive and transformative free-flowing force.

PERSONAL HEALTH PROFILE

As with everything in their lives, Sagittarians are apt to take a philosophical approach to their health. You seek to find the deeper meaning in all things. With *why* as one of your favorite words, you may question, for example, *why* you may experience certain health challenges or *why* one wellness approach works more effectively for you than another. This inquiring nature that pursues insightful answers is elemental to a Sagittarian's ability to live a full and healthful life.

Rather than relying solely on health-care practitioners for wellness wisdom, Sagittarians seek it from a large sphere of resources. From friends to co-workers, health books to spiritual texts, Archers aim to find a framework that will allow them access to truth and significance, the Sagittarian Holy Grail.

While a Sagittarian's spirited approach to living brings much pleasure, it may also pose health challenges. For example, being so enthusiastic, it is sometimes hard for you to acknowledge your limits. This can result in exhaustion or even reckless injuries, both avoidable by taking a slower, more deliberate approach to the task at hand.

Sagittarians love to celebrate any occasion—including just the adventure of another day—and these festivities often involve food and drink. If not enjoyed in moderation (a concept that doesn't come easily to the Archer), you may be prone to weight issues, especially later in life. Additionally, drinking alcohol and consuming fatty foods may pose extra challenges to your liver, an organ associated with your sign.

While your abundant energy and fiery constitution normally provide you with a strong sense of health, when you do fall ill, take comfort in the fact that you have amazing healing resources at hand. In addition to the deep level of understanding you seek, you always set your sights high and pursue your goals with gusto. If optimal well-being is your aim, as a Sagittarian, you'll travel far and wide to find the ways to achieve it. When combined with your profound level of faith, you hold an almost magical recipe for overcoming many wellness obstacles.

 ## AREAS OF HEALTH FOCUS

Each zodiac sign is associated with certain parts of the body. These may be inherent areas of vulnerability, but when attended to, they can become areas of strength. The parts of the body associated with Sagittarius include the following:

★ The **liver**, the body's largest organ, responsible for detoxifying chemicals, producing fat-digesting bile, and numerous other vital functions

★ The **thighs** and **buttocks**, both necessary for journeying and locomotion

★ The **hips**, **sacrum**, and **coccyx**, which provide you with stability and movement

★ The **sciatic nerve**, the longest and widest nerve, which runs from the lower back all the way to the feet

Your Sagittarian spirited energy, deep well of faith, and motivation to learn new things are some of the resources you can use when facing any health challenge.

Love Your Liver

Just like the god Jupiter, the Sagittarius-ruled liver performs numerous functions to maintain order, all in the name of supporting well-being. These include the filtration of blood, the detoxification of chemicals, the production of fat-metabolizing bile, and the storage of glycogen (a source of energy). One important way to support hepatic health is to reduce the burden placed on the liver's detoxification systems. To do so, watch your intake of alcohol and synthetic food additives, and choose organic over conventionally grown produce whenever you can. Also to this end, reduce your reliance on synthetically based household cleaners, opting for their more natural counterparts instead.

Strengthen Your Muscles

The sign of Sagittarius represents the desire to move from place to place, exploring the world and learning all that it has to teach. Consequently, it makes sense that in medical astrology, the buttocks and thighs, two related areas intimately connected to movement, are associated with your sign. If the muscles located in these areas—notably the quadriceps, hamstrings, or gluteus muscles—are overly tight or weak, it can lead to lower back pain, knee instability, or sciatic nerve impingement. Regular exercise and massage can keep your muscles toned. Also, if you have a desk job, honor your Sagittarian need to move, and walk around every hour or so to rev up the blood flow in your lower body.

Stabilize Hip Health

Symbols of female sexuality as well as fertility, the hips are another Sagittarius-ruled area of the body central to locomotion. An assortment of conditions—including arthritis, osteoporosis, and hamstring strains—can affect the hips' range of motion and cause pain. Exercise approaches that strengthen and stabilize the hip socket and surrounding muscles can be beneficial; these include Pilates, with its focus on muscle lengthening, and Gyrotonics, with its focus on joint mobilization. Additionally, making sure your diet is rich in bone-building nutrients—such as calcium, magnesium, and vitamin D—can help prevent osteoporosis in the hips.

Avoid Sports Injuries

Engaging in sports and fitness is a great outlet for a Sagittarian's abundant physical energy and competitive nature. Yet it's also an arena in which the Archer needs to take extra care. Enthusiastic Sagittarians are known to push themselves beyond their limits ("limits, what limits?"). This can put you at risk for strains, sprains, and other sports-related injuries. Don't forget to warm up and cool down before and after exercise, which is especially important as you age. Also, keep yourself well hydrated and nourished. These tips will help transform your athletic pursuits into feats of glory rather than bouts of injury.

 HEALTHY EATING TIPS

Enjoying food and drink is one means by which Sagittarians enthusiastically participate in the joyful adventure called life. Yet with great exuberance may come a tendency toward overindulgence, something the Archer should keep tabs on.

Enjoy Liver-Supporting Foods

Foods that maintain liver health include those rich in sulfur, such as onions, garlic, and the brassica vegetables (for example, cauliflower, kale, and broccoli). For optimal hepatic health, you'll also want to limit your consumption of alcohol, high-fat foods, synthetic additives, and foods grown with pesticides, since the liver has to work overtime to break down these compounds.

★ Onions go great in just about anything from soups to salads, chicken entrées to tofu stir-fries. Garlic and lemon, mixed with a touch of extra virgin olive oil, is a delicious liver-supporting dressing to top lightly steamed brassica vegetables. "Mocktails" are delightful non-alcoholic beverage alternatives for a festive Sagittarian to enjoy.

Don't Eat on the Run

With so many paths to pursue and adventures to experience, a Sagittarian's schedule is brimming with appointments, social engagements, and activities. As such, the Archer often noshes on the run, which can create challenges to eating healthfully. By not planning out meals, nourishment can often mean grabbing what's convenient and on hand, which is more than likely something that's packaged, processed, and laden with carbs.

★ Take the time to prepack snacks when you know you will be on the go all day. This will help you tide over your appetite and not give in to impulsive food choices. Some ideas include cut-up broccoli, baby carrots, trail mix, bananas, and organic energy bars.

Explore Culinary Globe-Trotting

Sagittarians are the travelers of the zodiac. Even if you aren't able to traverse the world physically, one way to experience the glories of the globe is to sample the unique food offerings of different cultures. By exploring international cuisines—whether by eating at ethnic restaurants or learning to cook these foods yourself—you'll expand your horizons and learn new things, the raisons d'être of any Sagittarian.

★ Embark on your culinary trek by visiting a bookstore and exploring its selection of world cuisine recipe books. Take a cooking class at a local community college, adult learning center, or natural foods market, and learn how to make tapas, mix curry blends, or prepare dim sum.

HEALTH-SUPPORTING FOODS

Many healthy foods—including olives and hazelnuts—are associated with your sign in medical astrology. Appreciative of other cultures' wisdom, Sagittarians would do well to incorporate the South American grains quinoa and amaranth into their diets.

Olives and Olive Oil

Sports-loving Sagittarians may be interested to know that olive wreaths and olive oil were some of the prizes awarded to ancient Olympic athletes. Today Jupiter-ruled olives and their oil still earn a gold medal when it comes to nutrition. Rich in health-promoting fats and antioxidants, olives and olive oil play a starring role in the Mediterranean diet and are thought to be one of the reasons that this approach to eating offers protection against cardiovascular disease and cancer.

★ Sampling different varieties of olives—Kalamata, Picholine, Cerignola, and Manzanilla, to name just a few—can be a delicious adventure. Opt for extra virgin oil as it has the highest concentration of antioxidants.

Hazelnuts

If wisdom comes with age, then Jupiter-ruled hazelnuts are a very intelligent food. Ancient Greek physicians praised the curative properties of hazelnuts. And even further back in time, close to five thousand years ago, the Chinese considered hazelnuts to be a very sacred food. Their track record for health-giving properties continues to this day, as they are a very rich source of many nutrients, including magnesium, manganese, vitamin E, and monounsaturated fat.

★ Toss hazelnuts onto salads or add to trail mix. For a Spanish twist on a pesto recipe, substitute hazelnuts and Manchego cheese for the pine nuts and Parmesan. Hazelnut oil has a high smoke point, making it a perfect choice for sautés and stir-fries.

Quinoa and Amaranth

Sagittarians looking for a sustained energy boost—whether for exercise or just life's daily adventures—should try quinoa and amaranth. These ancient foods—revered by the Incan, Mayan, and Aztec cultures—are rich in complex carbohydrates and fiber. Enjoyed like whole grains, quinoa and amaranth are unique in that they feature a well-rounded supply of all the essential amino acids, making them a good source of protein.

★ Before cooking quinoa, wash it well to remove its saponin compound, which can impart a soapy taste to this otherwise delicious food. Add two parts water to one part quinoa, and simmer for about fifteen minutes. Amaranth has a porridgelike texture, so you may want to cook it with brown rice if you'd like to enjoy a dish with a more grainlike consistency.

SPA AND WELLNESS THERAPIES

Spa and wellness therapies can be an active and engaging way to further your pursuit of well-being.

Thai Massage

If you seek a style of bodywork that's suited to your spirited temperament and appreciation for the wisdom of other cultures, try Thai massage. During a Thai massage session, you rest fully clothed on a padded floor mat while the practitioner stretches your muscles and mobilizes your joints by moving you into various yogalike postures. The practitioner then applies pressure—with his hands, feet, elbows, or knees—to release tension in your muscles and connective tissue.

★ In Thailand and other Asian countries, this form of bodywork is called *nuad phaen boran*. This translates into "ancient massage," a term you may see used to describe this healing art form.

Pilates

The enhanced strength and postural alignment that come from doing Pilates will help the Archer hold steady aim at any target on the horizon. During a Pilates session, you work with a trained instructor on a series of movement exercises, either on specialized machines or floor mats. In addition to core-strengthening benefits, Pilates fosters greater body awareness and muscle control as well as healthier breathing habits.

★ Remember that not all instructors, including those that teach Pilates, have the same level of wisdom and knowledge to share. Before committing to a particular instructor, compare the background and experience of several.

Equine-Assisted Psychotherapy

If, in your quest to better understand yourself, you've been considering psychotherapy, you may be interested in exploring Equine-Assisted Psychotherapy (EAP). Led by a trained mental health counselor and featuring horses to facilitate therapeutic benefit, EAP is especially well suited to Sagittarians, as your sign is symbolized by the mythic centaur. Through interacting with and caring for the horse, you can build self-confidence, enhance your nurturing spirit, and learn new relationship skills.

★ To find programs in your area, visit the website of the Equine Assisted Growth and Learning Association at www.eagala.org. In addition to EAP, there are forms of equine-assisted programs—such as hippotherapy—that focus on improving functional movement skills rather than psychotherapeutic healing.

RELAXATION PRACTICES

As Sagittarians are so adept at using their minds, imaginations, and active spirits to attract that which they seek, attaining relaxation may be a simple quest.

Creative Visualization

Sagittarians have an uncanny ability to manifest good fortune; it is as if your positive attitude, expansive vision, and unequivocal faith constituted a secret recipe for attracting treasured outcomes. With this ability, you would be a natural at creative visualization, a stress-relieving technique that engages your conscious and subconscious minds to work in unison to help you meet your chosen goals.

★ There are many books and audio books available to help you learn creative visualization techniques. Not only can this relaxation practice inspire calm, but you can also use it to achieve other goals, such as enhancing athletic performance or reducing muscular tension.

Travel

Let your arrow fly and follow it on a journey around the world. Exploring foreign countries—connecting with different land-scapes and the people who call them home—can be a very enriching experience for a Sagittarian. However, if budgetary or other lifestyle realities keep you from globe-trotting, you can still experience some of its benefits by reading travel memoirs and guidebooks or exploring travel-oriented television shows or films.

★ The message boards of travel websites can be great resources for information on hotels, restaurants, and tourist destinations. Television stations abound with inspiring shows on adventure travel, culinary expeditions, and sightseeing trips around the world.

Sports-Training Programs

Being active is more relaxing to a Sagittarian than sitting still, which is great since exercise is one of the best ways to reduce stress. Yet destination-oriented Sagittarians need a mission, and so exercising just for its own sake is unlikely to sustain your interest. To get fit while honoring your purposeful nature, pick a goal—whether it be completing a 5K walkathon, reducing your golf handicap, or getting in shape for ski season—and focus your fitness routine with this aim in mind.

★ Many gyms offer conditioning classes targeted toward different sports. If you are not careful, Sagittarian exuberance can lead to mishaps, so be realistic about what you are capable of doing at any one time to avoid sustaining injuries while you exercise.

YOGA POSES

Sagittarians love to learn, and yoga can provide you with an unending experience of discovering new postures, spiritual insights, and ways of being mindful in your practice.

Warrior II Pose (*Virabhadrasana II*)

Within the expansively open posture that characterizes Warrior II Pose, you can see the speculative nature of the Archer. In this posture, you gaze into the distance over your outstretched arm, peacefully visualizing a goal that lies ahead just over the horizon.

★ Stand tall with your arms outstretched to each side and your palms facing down. Walk your feet about four feet apart, rotating your right foot out 90 degrees and your left foot in about 30 degrees. Ensure that your heels are in the same line. Bend your right knee so it is above your right foot, and point your kneecap toward your middle toe. Extend your arms wide, stretching your shoulder blades while at the same time gazing over the top of your right fingertips. Stay in the pose for up to one minute, and then repeat on the other side.

Fire Log Pose (*Agnistambhasana*)

With the hips as an area of focus for fiery Sagittarians, the intense, hip-opening Fire Log Pose can be very beneficial for the Archer. This posture stretches the hip flexors as well as the gluteus and piriformis muscles.

★ Sit on your mat with your knees bent in front of you and the soles of your feet on the ground. Outwardly rotate your right hip so the outside of your right leg falls toward the floor. Adjust your right leg so your shin is parallel to the front of your mat. Place your left ankle on your right knee, with your left shin stacked above your right. If your

164 ★ planetary apothecary

left knee doesn't reach your right foot, place padding below it for support. Flex your feet and sit up straight. Stay in the pose for up to two minutes, and then switch leg positions.

High Lunge Pose (*Utthita ashwa sanchalanasana*)

High Lunge Pose lengthens the Sagittarius-ruled quadriceps and psoas muscles. It also teaches an important pearl of yogic wisdom: no matter how many times you do a pose, even one as basic as this, you can always learn new things about your body and breath.

★ Stand tall with your feet together, placing your hands on your hips. Bend forward at your hip joints, bring your palms to the floor in front of your feet, and gently bend your knees. Step your right foot back toward the edge of the mat. Bend your left knee so that it aligns over your ankle. Your hands (or fingertips) should be on the ground on either side of your left foot and your torso should be straight while you lean on your left thigh. Straighten the right leg by pushing strongly through your heel. Try to keep your hips even and allow them to sink toward the floor. Stay in the pose for up to one minute, and then repeat on the other side.

AROMATHERAPY

That aromatherapy is a healing tradition used by cultures worldwide and features the essential oils of plants from around the globe should make it attractive to internationally interested Sagittarians.

Juniper (*Juniperus communis*)

Juniper essential oil has far-reaching health benefits for a Sagittarian, including helping to relieve both muscle cramps and the uncomfortable feeling that comes from overindulging in food and drink. Throughout history, it has also been used in a number of wellness applications; for example, in ancient Greece, juniper was recognized by noted physicians as a powerful liver tonic while also being used by Olympic athletes to enhance endurance.

★ Add some juniper to massage oil for an after-exercise muscle-relieving salve. To give your energy levels a boost after a night of Sagittarian regaling, use juniper oil in a room diffuser, and revel in its uplifting and detoxifying properties.

Grapefruit (*Citrus paradisi*)

The essential oil of grapefruit is paradise for a Sagittarian on a wellness quest. It helps relieve muscle tension and is a good remedy for quelling joint pain. Grapefruit oil is also said to release stagnant liver chi (energy), which, according to traditional Chinese medicine, contributes to irritability as well as PMS. Additionally, it helps with fluid retention and may even reduce the cellulite that can appear on the Sagittarius-ruled thighs and buttocks.

★ Apply massage cream scented with grapefruit oil to your hips and thighs if they are beset with aches and pains. A belly balm of grapefruit essence mixed with coconut oil may help with bloating and liver detoxification.

Nutmeg (*Myristica fragrans*)

Nutmeg has long been a symbol of the Sagittarian attributes of good fortune. And, as luck would have it, nutmeg also has some great health benefits. Nutmeg helps allay muscle aches, inspires the mind, and enhances the vividness of dreams. According to medical folklore, people carried nutmeg in their pockets to relieve lower back pain.

★ Carry a vial of nutmeg oil in your pocketbook or briefcase. Not only will this twist on the folkloric tradition provide you with a talisman, but it will also make it easily accessible for times when your mind needs a bit of uplift and expansion. Use nutmeg oil judiciously since large doses may cause side effects.

NATURAL REMEDIES

The quest of a Sagittarian is that of discovery. Sorting through the multitude of available natural remedies to determine the ones that are best for you can be a very health-rewarding journey.

Milk Thistle (*Silybum marianum*)

Used since Greco-Roman times, milk thistle is currently one of the most commonly utilized remedies for liver health. Its popularity stems from its efficacy at providing the Sagittarius-ruled liver with a wide range of benefits. It serves as an aegis, protecting the liver from exposure to harmful toxins. Milk thistle is also a powerful antioxidant that protects the liver from free radical damage.

★ Milk thistle is commonly available in capsule and liquid tincture form. As many of its benefits have been attributed to its silymarin flavonoids, look for milk thistle remedies standardized to 70 to 80 percent of these compounds.

Choline

Choline—a B vitamin found in soy foods, egg yolks, and lentils—is a nutrient that offers benefits to the liver as well as other aspects of health. Dietary choline deficiency may lead to fat accumulation in the liver, which can cause inflammation and cell damage if severe. In addition, as a key component of neurons as well as the nervous system messenger acetylcholine, it plays a role in brain health.

★ Choline is available in a variety of forms including phosphatidylcholine, lecithin, and choline salt (such as choline chloride or bitartrate). For best absorption, take with meals.

Amla (*Emblica officinalis*)

If your quest to discover leads you to amla, you're in luck. One of the prized rejuvenating herbs in India and its Ayurvedic medical tradition, amla is said to promote longevity, referred to as the "sustainer" in traditional Hindu texts. Not only does amla contain more vitamin C than oranges, it is also used in Ayurvedic medicine as a liver tonic, a digestive strengthener, an immune system fortifier, and a hair conditioner.

★ Amla is available in either capsule or powder form. You may also find dried amla fruit or pickled preserves in stores that sell Indian food.

FLOWER ESSENCES

Wisdom-seeking Sagittarians may appreciate flower essences for their ability to teach you more about yourself, since they can help you understand and overcome some of the stress you may experience. All flower essences can be used similarly: mix a few drops in a glass of water, and drink several times a day; add some to a bath; or place in a water-filled mister bottle to enhance your environment.

Sage (*Salvia officinalis*)

A Sagittarian rarely misses the forest for the trees; rather, the opposite sometimes proves challenging. With your focus on the big picture, you may at times miss the smaller details, thus forgoing additional learning and insight opportunities. When surveying life experiences, if you need some assistance probing your memory for nuances and subtleties that can yield a greater level of understanding, try Sage flower essence.

Vervain (*Verbena officinalis*)

Sagittarians are passionate, especially about their ideals and the pursuit of their aspirations. Energetic and charismatic, you push yourself toward great accomplishments. Yet, sometimes you may set overly optimistic goals for yourself, which can put you en route to physical exhaustion and nervous tension. When you need to balance your arduous pursuits with a pragmatic perspective, try Vervain flower essence.

Angelica (*Angelica archangelica*)

Sagittarians are known for their deep faith, their trust that everything has meaning and import, and that every situation eventually works itself out for the greater good. Even so, your faith may be challenged for periods of time, notably during a crisis or important life transition. For guidance during these times, and assistance in restoring your belief in an ordered benevolence, try Angelica flower essence.

capricorn

SUN IN CAPRICORN ★ December 22–January 20

CHARACTERISTICS ★ Loyal / Hardworking / Pragmatic / Structured / Ambitious / Classy / Frugal / Disciplined / Committed / Persistent / Sarcastic / Conservative

SYMBOL ★ The *Mountain Goat*, an animal known for its perseverance, sure-footedness, and dedicated guardianship of its resources. In mythological and cultural traditions, the Mountain Goat is a symbol of prosperity, fertility, and the beneficial elements of nature.

PLANETARY RULER ★ *Saturn*, the planet famous for its intricately structured orbiting rings. Saturn was the Roman god of agriculture, renowned for his leadership and for introducing social order and codes of government to civilization. His counterpart in Greek mythology was Kronos. In astrology, Saturn represents time, limitations, rules, and responsibilities, all integral aspects of the ability to turn ideas into reality.

ELEMENT ★ *Earth*, characterized by the grounded energy of creativity, resistance, and practicality. It is fertile and passive, and it relates to the world on a sensual level.

QUALITY ★ *Cardinal*, which represents the initiation of the creative cycle. It reflects ambition, enterprise, speed, and a self-starting force that propels energy into the world.

Capricorns thrive on accomplishing goals. So if you set wellness as one of your aims, you'll strive hard to achieve it. With ardent strength in the face of adversity, you are not likely to complain about your health or any aches and pains you may feel. While others may try to elicit sympathy when sick, not Capricorns, whose self-reliant nature likes to maintain a sense of public composure. This may work well to help you power through the limitations that would stop others. Yet a great source of your personal healing can come from knowing that sometimes other people's knowledge and experience can benefit you and that asking for help isn't necessarily a sign of weakness.

As Capricorns don't like to sway much from tradition, when it comes to health care, you're more inclined to follow mainstream, society-sanctioned approaches that boast long, successful track records and a litany of research-based benefits. It's not that you won't try alternative wellness therapies; it's just that you are not the one first jumping on the bandwagon of the newest trends. Yet, once you have tried a new natural remedy or therapy and find that it works well for you, you will readily include it as an integral part of your wellness regimen. After all, loyalty is one of the hallmarks of your astrological sign.

Frugal Capricorns should realize that it's possible to be budget conscious and health conscious at the same time. Some of the best things in life, and health care, are free (including stress-relieving techniques such as exercise and meditation) or relatively low cost (such as a whole foods diet). Many insurance companies also offer wellness therapy benefits for massage, chiropractic, and acupuncture, so the out-of-pocket expenses for these services may be minimal. And remember the old maxim, "An ounce of prevention is worth (at least) a pound of cure."

With your planetary ruler, Saturn, representing limitations and delays, life may be challenging for Capricorns until you reach your forties, a time when you gracefully hit your stride. It's as if all that hard work you did in your early adulthood finally pays off, with a youthful sense of maturity as the prize.

 AREAS OF HEALTH FOCUS

Each zodiac sign is associated with certain parts of the body. These may be inherent areas of vulnerability, but when attended to, they can become areas of strength. The parts of the body associated with Capricorn include the following:

★ The **skeletal system**—including the **bones**, **cartilage**, and **teeth**—that provide you with structure

★ The **joints**, in general, and the **knees**, in particular, the bending of which is integral to your ability to move forward in the world

★ The **skin**, the protective barrier that encompasses and defines your form

Your Capricorn persistence, strategic approach to getting things accomplished, and committed work ethic are some of the resources you can use when facing any health challenge.

Keep Your Knees Flexible

In medical astrology, the sign of Capricorn is associated with the joints, the strength and flexibility of which allow you to move fluidly through the world. As such, you may want to take special care of your joints—especially your knees—to ward off the potential for developing arthritis. Characterized by cartilage and synovial membrane degeneration, arthritis can lead to pain, swelling, and restricted movement. An anti-inflammatory diet—filled with foods and spices rich in omega-3 fatty acids and antioxidants—can do wonders for supporting rheumatic health, as can watching your stress levels. And speaking of stress, the knees have to support a force equal to about three times your body weight; therefore, shedding any excess pounds can help reduce the risk of experiencing arthritis in this Capricorn-ruled joint.

Support Skin Health

The structure and integrity of the skin is under the auspices of your sign in medical astrology. As such, it may be an area of vulnerability, making it even more important to take extra good care of your skin, protecting it against dryness, breakouts, and rashes. A practical approach to skin health involves following a supportive diet that includes antioxidant-rich fruits and vegetables, omega-3–rich fish and seeds, and filtered water. Investigating whether common food allergens, like dairy and wheat, are contributing to any skin problems you may have (such as dermatitis or acne) is also a good strategy. Additionally, watch out for topical allergies that can be provoked by everyday products such as lotions, cleansers, and laundry detergents.

Avoid Burnout

Even though your sign is known for its endurance, Capricorns tend to work so hard pursuing their objectives that they run the risk of running themselves into the ground. As an earth sign, you do have an incredible storehouse of physical resources. Yet, like any other inventory, if it's not replenished, there's a chance you can deplete your stock. If you don't acknowledge your limits, your body will just do it for you, using a cold or other illness as a signal to make you stop and rest. Be proactive and build relaxation time into your schedule. This will make your work life (as well as the rest of your life) more productive and enjoyable.

Work on Reducing Anxiety

Capricorns take their careers and contributions to society very seriously. You invest great effort in whatever you do, priding yourself on your reputation and how the world sees you. But, as the taskmasters of the zodiac, if you don't feel that you're measuring up to your high ideals, you may descend into feelings of depression or anxiety. If your work isn't working for your mental health, it may be time to retool your attitude and approach. For example, make sure that your aims can be realistically attained in the time frame envisioned. Also, survey your goals and see whether they truly bring you personal satisfaction or just fulfill someone else's desires for your life.

 HEALTHY EATING TIPS

As one who cherishes the rules of the natural world, it's common sense to a Capricorn that eating whole foods can provide your body with the nutrients it needs to function optimally—and therefore, for your health to flourish.

Make Healthy Eating a Top Priority

As an earth sign, Capricorns are well connected to their bodies, including their sense of hunger and need for nourishment. Yet if you become engrossed in a project—no matter how big or small—you may ignore your hunger and put off eating. If this means meals are delayed a few minutes, that's not a problem. But when it verges on hours, it can wreak havoc on your blood sugar and compromise your sense of well-being.

★ Remember that keeping yourself well nourished is as, if not more, important than any other project that captures your attention. In fact, you'll probably get fresh inspiration if you're not distracted by the ornery mood that hunger pangs can produce. Keep nuts, trail mix, or energy bars at your desk or in your car as a time-saving way to keep your energy on track during your busy days.

Bone Up on a Healthy Diet

Diet can play an integral role in promoting the health of your bones. It's important to know both what to eat—foods rich in calcium, vitamin D, and magnesium—and also what not to eat. Limit caffeine, refined sugar, salt, and phosphates (found in colas) as they can leech calcium from bones, weakening its structural matrix.

★ As a stand-in for coffee, consider drinking green tea. Not only does it have about one-fourth the caffeine, but research suggests that its catechin phytonutrients, notably EGCG, can help increase bone mineral density. Alternatives to cola abound: look for natural fruit-flavored sodas, or make your own at home by mixing sparkling water with fruit juice.

Drink Water

Capricorns are notoriously bad at drinking enough water. Why? It's probably the same reason that you put off eating—you don't want to divert your attention from the activity at hand. Yet it only takes seconds to sip water: a great investment of time that will yield numerous health benefits.

★ To save yourself time going to the water cooler, fill up a few bottles in the morning, and keep them at your desk (room temperature water is better for your digestion anyway). Look for stainless steel or glass water bottles; this way you can avoid exposure to the estrogen-disrupting BPA chemical found in some plastic ones.

HEALTH-SUPPORTING FOODS

Mountain Goats can incorporate many delicious foods into their diets to help promote the health of their Capricorn-ruled bones. These include goat's milk, leafy green vegetables, and foods rich in vitamin D, such as salmon and sardines.

Goat's Milk

Unsurprisingly, goat's milk—and the yogurt and cheese made from it—can be a health-supporting food for the Mountain Goat. It is rich in calcium, with 1 cup providing over 300 milligrams of this bone-building mineral. Take note if you have dairy allergies: many people who can't tolerate cow's milk do just fine with goat's milk.

★ Add goat cheese (also known as chèvre) to a salad, sandwich, or cheese plate. While goat cheese is readily available, goat's milk and yogurt may be more difficult to find in supermarkets. Natural food stores and farmers' markets are your best bets for these tart and refreshing foods.

Leafy Greens

While leafy greens appear delicate, they can actually form the backbone of a diet that supports the Capricorn-ruled bones. Not only do these greens—such as kale, chard, spinach, and collard greens—contain large amounts of calcium, but unlike dairy products, they're also concentrated in bone-strengthening nutrients such as magnesium, vitamin K, and manganese. Additionally, with their abundance of antioxidants that fight cartilage-damaging free radicals, they can make a great contribution to joint health.

★ While it's true that leafy greens contain oxalic acid, the ability of this compound to inhibit calcium absorption is minimal enough to still make these foods an important source of this mineral. Quickly steaming greens—for no more than five minutes—will help retain many nutrients that would be otherwise lost to overcooking.

Vitamin D–Rich Foods

Vitamin D has long been known for benefiting the Capricorn-ruled bones, with a deficiency of this important nutrient linked to osteoporosis. Recently, it has also shown health-promoting promise for hypertension, diabetes, depression, and multiple sclerosis. While sun exposure produces vitamin D in the body, ensuring you get adequate amounts through your diet is important. This is notably true for hardworking Capricorns, who, often tied to their desks, may not see the light of day nearly enough.

★ Fish such as salmon, cod, sardines, and mackerel are some of the richest sources of vitamin D. Cow's milk is fortified with this sunshine nutrient as well, although cheese and yogurt generally are not. If your diet doesn't provide you with enough vitamin D, consider taking it in supplement form.

SPA AND WELLNESS THERAPIES

Don't let Capricornian frugality stop you from enjoying spa and wellness therapies, notably as they are great investments for your health.

Swedish Massage

A Capricorn likes things that function well: easy access and a proven track record are a plus; exotic bells and whistles, not so much. Therefore, Swedish massage—the classic form offered at most spas and health clinics—may serve well as the bodywork of choice for a pragmatic Capricorn. Swedish massage relieves stress and muscular tension as well as symptoms—such as pain and reduced range of motion—associated with arthritis of the Capricorn-ruled knee joint.

★ To get the most from a massage, temper your normal Capricornian reserve and communicate to the practitioner what your body needs and the amount of pressure that feels best. Find practitioners through referrals, or go to the directory of the Associated Bodywork and Massage Professionals at www.massagetherapy.com.

Body-Moisturizing Treatments

As Capricorns need to pay special attention to their skin—keeping it healthy and well hydrated—body-moisturizing treatments can make a great addition to a wellness portfolio. These spa treatments usually begin with exfoliation. This step preps your skin to absorb moisture both during the treatment and afterwards. Then a deeply hydrating body mask is applied. Some spas even offer body-moisturizing treatments made from goat's milk, an über-Capricornian treat.

★ Body-moisturizing therapies are a complement to, rather than a substitute for, an everyday routine of cleansing and hydration. For an at-home approach, apply a deeply nourishing body lotion after scrubbing your body with a loofah or dry brush.

Feldenkrais Method

Ingrained movement patterns—even the ones of a typically efficient Capricorn—are often damaging to the body and can cause
pain and muscular tension. The Feldenkrais Method is a style
of body-awareness training that makes you more conscious of
any habitual movement patterns that may not best serve your
body's structure and function. Using verbal and light-touch
cues, Feldenkrais practitioners teach you to move more effi-
caciously, allowing you to enjoy reduced strain and increased
range of motion.

★ Feldenkrais is available in individual and group sessions. To find a
practitioner near you, go to www.feldenkrais.com. Additionally, some
yoga and dance studios offer classes in this movement-awareness
method, so inquire with those in your area.

 RELAXATION PRACTICES

For optimal health, Capricorns should work hard at incorporating
more relaxation time into their schedule.

Hiking

Emanate your astrological totem, and climb a mountain (or even
just a hill). Hiking is a great way to get some exercise, enjoy
the fresh air, and get in touch with nature. If the weather is too
inclement for a hike, don't despair; there's always the gym's stair-
stepping machine or inclined elliptical trainer when you want an
activity that allows you to ascend, albeit virtually, a mountain.
Also, try out the bouldering wall at a rock climbing gym to see if
that piques your interest.

★ While many Capricorns like to keep to themselves, don't forget that you needn't climb any mountain (literally or figuratively) alone. Consider hiking with a partner, especially if you're concerned about safety.

Labyrinth Walking

Walking a labyrinth is a moving meditation with a destination, a differentiation that Capricorns will appreciate. The outward goal—to weave your way through the mazelike structure—naturally reinforces the inner goal of calming your mind and relaxing your body. Knowing that labyrinths are not a New Age creation but a time-honored tradition—the oldest, located on the island of Crete, is over four thousand years old—will appeal to legacy-honoring Capricorns.

★ Labyrinths can be found throughout the world; cathedrals, public parks, and healing centers are just some of the places that feature these meditative mandalas. To find one near you, go to the Labyrinth Society's website at www.labyrinthsociety.org.

Frolic and Play

All work and no play makes Jack a dull boy (and Jill a dull girl). While you're filling out your calendar with all of your tasks, projects, and deadlines, don't forget to schedule in some fun. While it may seem that you will achieve nothing by playing, a life that has levity and joy is, in itself, a great accomplishment that provides many rewards.

★ Release your inner child and head to the playground. Have fun and relieve stress by swinging on the ropes, balancing on the seesaw, and descending the slide with reckless—but careful—abandon.

YOGA POSES

Yoga can be a pragmatic way for a Capricorn to gain strength and flexibility. Look for a teacher who focuses on alignment to best safeguard joint health.

Mountain Pose (*Tadasana*)

Mastering Mountain Pose—a basic yoga posture that focuses on alignment and solidity—can help the Mountain Goat reach the top of any peak.

★ Stand with your feet together, big toes touching and heels slightly apart, and evenly distribute your weight through your soles. Lift your kneecaps by tightening your quadriceps muscles, and lengthen your tailbone toward the floor. Hug your shoulder blades into your back, and press them down while lengthening your neck and resting your arms at your sides. The crown of your head should float above the center of your body, and you should feel a strong line of energy from your feet all the way to the top of your head. Stay in the pose for up to one minute.

Chair Pose (*Utkatasana*)

Not only does the bending involved in Chair Pose promote flexibility and range of motion, but it also greatly strengthens the quadriceps muscles, supporting proper alignment of the Capricorn-ruled kneecaps.

★ Stand in Mountain Pose (see the previous description). Raise your arms overhead, with palms facing each other. Slowly bend your knees until your thighs are almost parallel to the ground. Your torso will naturally lean forward so that your body is in a somewhat zigzag position. Try to create a slight backbend in your upper back. Stay in the pose for up to one minute.

Hero Pose (*Virasana*)

Known for their many achievements and valiant characteristics, Capricorns definitely embody heroic qualities. Hero Pose is a great posture to bring flexibility to your knee and ankle joints.

★ Kneel on the floor, with your knees touching and your shins angling out so your feet are positioned wider than your hips. Rest the top of your ankles on the floor (if this position is painful, kneel on a folded blanket or mat). Slowly begin to sit back between your feet. As you do so, place your hands on your upper calves, and gently move the muscles to the outside to avoid compressing them. Point your feet straight back and not out to the side. Sit up tall with your shoulder blades descending down your back. Don't hesitate to use padding for your buttocks, knees, and ankles if needed. Stay in the pose for up to one minute at first, gradually working your way up to five minutes.

AROMATHERAPY

Aromatherapy embraces qualities elemental to a Capricorn as it is an easy-to-use, relatively inexpensive, and readily accessible wellness practice.

Cypress (*Cupressus sempervirens*)

The Saturn-ruled cypress tree is so strong that its wood was prized in antiquity and was used to construct ships and buildings. The fortitude of its essential oil, distilled from its leaves, is also well known in its own right. Especially good for soothing rheumatic pain and enhancing skin tone, cypress can also inspire calm in a Capricorn during times of grief and crisis.

★ Soak a small towel in a mixture of cypress and warm water, applying it as a compress to sore joints. During times of emotional upheaval, keep a cypress-scented handkerchief with you so you can readily inhale its soothing aroma.

Frankincense (genus *Boswellia*)

Frankincense has great skin-rejuvenating properties, an especially beneficial attribute for Capricorns, and a quality well regarded by the ancient Egyptians, who utilized it in their cosmetics. Applied topically, it can also be used for easing rheumatic pain. Not only valued for its practical uses, frankincense is also endowed with inspirational properties. It was one of the gifts of the magi, after all, and is commonly used in religious rites as well.

★ Add some frankincense to unscented body oil and massage into achy joints. Mix a drop or two into your moisturizer to enhance skin tone. Burn frankincense resin over incense charcoal to add a divine fragrance to your environment.

Scotch Pine (*Pinus sylvestris*)

Scotch pine is a great scent to use all year long, but especially during the winter season, including the months of December and January, when the Sun is in your sign. It kills fungus and other microbes that can compromise your home's air quality, a notable benefit when the cold weather keeps you indoors. Additionally, its exhilarating scent is just the ticket for lifting the winter blues.

★ Use Scotch pine in an aromatherapy diffuser to freshen the air. Blend with massage oil for a vitalizing muscle-relaxing treatment (but test on a small patch of skin first, as some people find that it irritates their skin).

Natural remedies can be a very smart and cost-effective way to promote wellness for Capricorns who appreciate intelligence and a great value.

Glucosamine Sulfate

Glucosamine sulfate is one of the most popular dietary supplements for relieving the symptoms of arthritis and improving the overall health of the Capricorn-ruled knees. Since it is a precursor of cartilage molecules, glucosamine strengthens this connective tissue rather than just providing symptomatic treatment like many over-the-counter anti-inflammatory medicines do. Research studies have found glucosamine sulfate reduces joint stiffness, swelling, and pain.

★ If you're watching your salt intake, look for glucosamine stabilized with potassium sulfate rather than sodium sulfate. Those with diabetes may want to check with their doctors before taking glucosamine since there's a possibility that the supplement can elevate blood sugar levels.

S-adenosylmethionine (SAMe)

SAMe (pronounced "SAM-me") is a naturally occurring compound derived from methionine, one of only two food-based amino acids that contain sulfur, a mineral associated with your planetary ruler, Saturn. SAMe's claim to fame is that it is one of the best methyl donors around, and since methylation is critical to so many body functions, its benefits are widespread. SAMe is thought to hold promise for alleviating the Capricorn-associated health conditions of arthritis and depression, as well as discouraging heart disease and age-related cognitive decline.

★ Don't take SAMe close to bedtime as its energy boost may inhibit sound sleep. For best absorption, look for supplements that are enteric-coated.

Turmeric

Since turmeric has an amazing array of health benefits, practical Capricorns would do well to add it to their medicine (or spice) cabinet. Abundant in the powerful antioxidant and anti-inflammatory compound curcumin, turmeric has been used in Ayurvedic and other traditional medical approaches to treat arthritis. Applied topically, turmeric may also help reduce acne and heal skin wounds.

★ While turmeric is available as a dietary supplement in capsule form, you can also buy the loose powder in the spice section of your market and use it in your cooking. Be careful when using it, though: while it can have an indelibly positive effect on your health, turmeric can also create an indelible stain on your clothes.

 FLOWER ESSENCES

Once a down-to-earth Capricorn sees how effective flower essences are at balancing emotional and psychological well-being, these remedies will become a regularly relied-upon facet of your wellness regimen. All flower essences can be used similarly: mix a few drops in a glass of water, and drink several times a day; add some to a bath; or place in a water-filled mister bottle to enhance your environment.

Mimulus (*Mimulus guttatus*)

Capricorns hold themselves to very high standards. The idea of failure—of not attaining one's sought-after goals—is one of the Mountain Goat's greatest fears. While you may be inclined to use this fear of failure as motivation, it can also undermine your ability to make objective judgments, impelling you to act from an emotional, rather than rational, space. Mimulus is an effective flower essence for inspiring courage and confidence, which, when partnered with your perseverance, is an unbeatable combination.

Vine (*Vitis vinifera*)

Confident Capricorns would rather lead than follow, knowing they can get the job done right. Yet keep in mind that too much persistent self-reliance can sometimes lead to a myopic vision of what others are capable of and the importance of their unique con-tributions. Vine flower essence is a good remedy to use when you need a reminder that delegating is not the sign of a weak leader but a powerful one who successfully empowers others.

Oak (*Quercus robur*)

While Capricorns set their sights high on all they want to achieve for themselves and those they love, it's important to realize that, in fact, one person is only capable of doing so much. (Capricorns are masters of burning the candle at both ends, but risk burning out.) Oak flower essence can help you gracefully surrender to your limits and more readily ask assistance from others. It proves a great stress reliever, helping diminish a tendency toward placing unrelenting demands on yourself.

aquarius

SUN IN AQUARIUS ★ January 21–February 18

CHARACTERISTICS ★ Cerebral / Altruistic / Egalitarian / Friendly / Philanthropic / Eccentric / Perceptive / Detached / Innovative / Progressive / Rebellious / Independent

SYMBOL ★ The *Water Bearer*, a figure who gathers wisdom and insight and offers it in service to the world. In mythological and cultural traditions, the Water Bearer sustains and advances life on Earth.

PLANETARY RULER ★ *Uranus*, the first planet discovered using telescope technology and known for its unique orbit. Uranus was the Greek god of the sky and was both son and husband of Gaia, the earth goddess. Reflecting Aquarius's inherent originality, Uranus is the only planet named after a Greek, rather than a Roman, god. In astrology, Uranus represents innovation, sudden revelations, unpredictability, and the chaos that is an integral part of a connected structure.

ELEMENT ★ *Air*, characterized by the agile energy of thoughts, observation, and logic. It is social, intellectual, changeable, and relationship oriented.

QUALITY ★ *Fixed*, which represents the planning and building phase of the creative cycle. It reflects reliability, predictability, and a disciplined force that persists in creating structure.

Aquarians possess great vitality. You maintain a dynamic energy and sense of composure that can translate into sustained good health.

Physical ailments generally seem to bother you less than they bother others. That's partially a result of your Aquarian altruistic nature: you are simply less concerned with yourself than about the welfare of others. It is also because, as an air sign, Aquarians are not very rooted in their bodies, living more in their highly perceptive minds, which they can use to their health advantage. For example, pay attention to any out-of-the-blue flashes of insight— which Aquarians regularly experience—that have to do with your well-being.

As a global citizen, you don't discriminate based on origins and are equally comfortable with those who come from across the ocean as down the street. This respect for other cultures may translate into a wellness regimen that resembles the United Nations: essential oils from India, foods from Brazil, relaxation practices from China. With a keen ability to perceive vibrations, you're likely to be attracted to energy medicine: while acupuncture, hands-on healing, and flower essences may seem "New Agey" to some, you tend to consider them timeless (and highly effective).

This openness to energy is also reflected in your highly charged internal circuitry and heightened ability to sense electromagnetic fields. Therefore, disruptions in your body's bioelectrical system (including your "aura") will be readily experienced as low-level interruptions in your sense of wellness, including energy depletion, irritability, and frazzled nerves. These disruptions are often caused by overexposure to the computers, cell phones, wireless PDAs, and other technological wizardry so ubiquitous in the modern world (and to which many Water Bearers are so attracted). For optimal Aquarian health, it's important to pull the plug on the information superhighway every now and then to keep your own internal circuitry humming properly.

Rebels at heart, Aquarians are not ones to submit to society-sanctioned authorities and, as such, many Water Bearers are equally comfortable getting their wellness needs met by an acupuncturist or naturopath as they are by a conventional medical doctor. Whichever type of health-care practitioner you choose, look for one who can see you as the complex and integrated individual that you are.

 ## AREAS OF HEALTH FOCUS

Each zodiac sign is associated with certain parts of the body. These may be inherent areas of vulnerability, but when attended to, they can become areas of strength. The parts of the body associated with Aquarius include the following:

★ The **lower legs**, including the **calf muscles**, **Achilles tendon**, and the **peripheral circulatory system**, which supplies them with blood

★ The **ankles**, the flexibility and structure of which allow for efficient movement

★ The **retina** of the eye, which provides you with vision

★ The **bioelectrical system**, the electromagnetic waves inherent in, and radiating from, all body cells

Your Aquarian keen mind, great intuitive awareness, and ability to see the big picture are some of the resources you can use when facing any health challenge.

Mind Your Lower Legs and Ankles

Just like the Greek hero Achilles, Aquarians are fearless warriors committed to fighting for their cause. And just like Achilles, your spot of vulnerability is the eponymous tendon, as well as the rest of your lower leg including your calf and ankle. Numerous afflictions can impact this area of the body including muscle spasms, shin splints, restless leg syndrome, and swollen or twisted ankles. As Aquarians are prone to experiencing the unexpected, take extra precautions when exercising to guard against injury. As for diet, magnesium- and potassium-rich foods, including fruits and vegetables, can help keep your muscles functioning smoothly.

Prevent Varicose Veins

Your sign's rebellious nature extends to the workings of the body as well, with Aquarius ruling physiological actions that go against the natural gradient. One such example is the peripheral blood circulation, notably the action of the Aquarius-ruled calves to pump blood back from the lower body to the heart in an action that defies gravity. If this function isn't working properly, it can manifest in varicose veins. While a doctor should be consulted to rule out the more serious chronic venous insufficiency condition that can compromise overall health, there are some general self-care treatments that can benefit leg health. For example, walk regularly to stimulate circulation, apply a compress of witch hazel to your legs, and consider vein-strengthening herbs such as butcher's broom, horse chestnut, or gotu kola.

Protect Your Vision

Aquarians are visionaries, blessed with an ability to sense a cohesive pattern and imagine the paths that will lead our present world into a more altruistic future. Your sign is also associated with vision—the sense of sight, that is—since it not only governs the retina but also the process of perceiving and translating light waves into images. You can take care of your eyes in numerous ways including wearing UV ray–blocking sunglasses and eating a diet that includes fish, carotenoid-rich fruits and vegetables, and leafy greens. A good multivitamin can also help you cover all your bases when it comes to the numerous nutrients that support optimal eye health.

Recharge Your Internal Circuitry

Aquarians possess a large sensory radar screen, which allows them to perceive a greater degree of stimuli, including subtle energies and vibrations. While this gives you access to greater perceptions than most, it may also overtax your nervous system at times, which may lead to feelings of restlessness, anxiety, and exhaustion. To pacify your internal circuitry, take time away from technology every once in a while (for example, make Sunday a day of rest from the computer). Spending time outdoors can also help you resonate with the more harmonious vibrations of nature. Additionally, a whole foods diet can benefit the nervous system with several nutrients—including omega-3 fats, vitamin B6, and folate—playing especially important roles in promoting nerve health.

HEALTHY EATING TIPS

Less in their bodies than in their minds, Aquarians need to ensure that they don't overlook the importance of a healthy diet for their physical and mental well-being.

Eat Raw and Grounding Foods

Eating fresh, raw foods keeps Aquarians buzzing, providing you with the life-force energy that helps your mind stay resonant and astutely aware of the subtleties of your environment. Yet an overreliance on raw foods can make you feel ungrounded. The solution: eat fruit, enjoy vegetables in both their raw and lightly cooked forms, and include a range of grounding foods such as nuts, beans, and whole grains in your diet.

★ An easy way to ensure you're eating fresh, raw foods is to enjoy a salad at lunch and/or dinner. Quickly cooking vegetables—most can be steamed in five minutes—preserves nutrients and also saves valuable time. That's a plus for an Aquarian, as you would rather be out saving the world than spending extra time in the kitchen.

Choose Foods That Benefit Circulation

With Aquarius associated with the peripheral circulatory system and lower legs, eating a diet to promote the integrity of your veins and capillaries is central to elevating your health. While all nutrients are important, the antioxidants—including vitamins C and E and flavonoids—are particularly beneficial when it comes to buttressing blood vessels and helping to avoid varicose veins.

★ While most people think of oranges as the premier source of vitamin C, guavas, strawberries, papaya, and kiwifruit actually contain more of this powerful antioxidant on a per calorie basis. Sunflower seeds, almonds, mustard greens, and olives are all rich in vitamin E. And anytime you see a purple- or red-colored fruit or vegetable, it is a good bet that it is filled with flavonoid phytonutrients.

Honor Your Need for Freedom

Aquarians thrive on freedom. You want to be free to do what you want to do when you want to do it. This includes eating. While others may subscribe to a regular routine, eating according to expectations goes against your independent nature. So honor the nonconformist in you, and eat to the beat of your own mealtime drum.

★ Give yourself the liberty to eat when it seems right to do so. While Aquarians are not always in tune with what *feels* nourishing for their bodies, use your perceptive mind to *know* what would be nurturing; look for signs and signals—such as if your nervous system feels a bit frayed—that will help you tailor your meal patterns.

HEALTH-SUPPORTING FOODS

There are many foods Aquarians can choose that can help them sustain their energetic stability. Some beneficial ones for the Water Bearer include exotic fruits, lutein- and zeaxanthin-rich foods, and green tea.

Exotic Fruit

Aquarians are the global citizens of the zodiac, and as such, they find the exotic both attractive and familiar. That's of benefit when it comes to fruits, as those from the tropics—such as goji and açai berries, guava, and even the more common papaya and pineapple— can be health-promoting additions to an Aquarian diet.

★ Goji berries are rich in vision health–promoting zeaxanthin and can be enjoyed as part of an energy-boosting trail mix. Anthocyanin-rich açai is available in juice form. In addition to the numerous vitamins and minerals they contain, papaya and pineapple also contain digestion-enhancing enzymes. Other exotic fruits—including vitamin C–rich guavas—can be found in Asian and natural food markets.

Lutein- and Zeaxanthin-Rich Foods

Lutein and zeaxanthin are related antioxidant carotenoids found concentrated in yellow-colored foods such as corn, winter squash, and egg yolks, as well as in deep green leafy vegetables. They can also be found in the retina and lens of your eyes, where they protect against sun-induced damage. Eating foods rich in these phytonutrients can help reduce your risk of developing cataracts and macular degeneration.

★ Add spinach to an omelet for a colorful and delicious breakfast. Winter squash has a sweet flavor and makes a great side dish. Cut into small cubes, it steams in less than ten minutes. While fresh corn is nutrient-rich, products made from it—such as corn oil and high-fructose corn syrup—are not.

Green Tea

Oscillating Aquarians like the buzz that caffeine provides. Yet too much caffeine—the amount provided by just two medium cups of coffee—can have a diuretic effect, pulling vital water from your body. So after your first cup of coffee, consider switching to antioxidant-rich green tea. It features about one-fourth the caffeine, yet it can provide you with steady energy throughout the day.

★ Green tea comes in many different varieties; the most popular are *sencha, hojicha, bancha,* and *genmaicha.* You can either brew it using loose leaves or tea bags. When making green tea, don't use boiling water—a below-simmer 170°F should be the maximum.

 SPA AND WELLNESS THERAPIES

With your global perspective, open-minded Aquarians appreciate how spa and wellness treatments from other cultures can be of great benefit.

Acupuncture

Aquarians will consider the virtue of a wellness technique even if it hasn't passed muster with society's traditional methods of assessing efficacy. Take acupuncture, for example, a system of healing that has yet to be "proven" by Western science but one whose inherent value the Aquarian mind can perceive. Acupuncture also speaks to your awareness that even if something is imperceptible, that doesn't mean it doesn't exist: the fact that health can be attained through balancing chi (subtle energy) by inserting needles along the body's invisible energy meridians seems as "real" to an Aquarian as anything else.

★ Acupuncture is performed by acupuncturists, health-care practitioners who receive years of education in this healing art. Medical doctors may also incorporate acupuncture into their practice after completing two to three hundred hours of training.

Reiki

Another wellness therapy that focuses on balancing vital energy is Reiki (pronounced "RAY-kee"), a type of hands-on healing practice. While meditating on different symbols, the practitioner transmits chi, which the recipient experiences as a warm flow of radiant energy. Reiki is great for stress reduction and relaxation and may also help relieve chronic pain.

★ If you like the experience of receiving Reiki, consider training in this healing method. It can be a great way to further connect with your own energy.

NIA Technique

Aquarians thrive in group situations that allow them to express their freedom and individuality. That's why the NIA technique—

an eclectic fitness system that's a combination of dance, martial arts, yoga, and movement therapy—is so well suited to your nature. NIA classes provide a flexible structure in which each participant has the autonomy to guide their own individual movement experiences. NIA not only tones and strengthens muscles and joints, but it also provides an energizing approach to balancing the nervous system.

★ NIA classes are taught at spas, fitness centers, and dance studios. To find a certified instructor, go to the NIA technique website at www.nianow.com.

RELAXATION PRACTICES

It is important for Aquarians to take time to recharge their batteries every now and again with activities that nurture both their mind and body.

Qigong

Qigong is a meditative movement practice that has many Aquarian characteristics, including an egalitarian- and community-oriented nature; for example, in its native land of China, young and old, rich and poor take part in qigong, with large classes occurring in public outdoor spaces. During this practice, you perform gentle movements that open your awareness to vibration fields within and around you. You also hone in on your sensory perception, which can become sharper and more precise over time.

★ There are numerous qigong books and DVDs available that describe the fundamentals of this mindfulness practice. Although you can practice qigong on your own, it is best to first learn proper techniques and movements from a skilled teacher in a class setting.

Mineral Salt Bath

The symbol for Aquarius is the Water Bearer, a figure who pours this life-sustaining liquid from an urn, offering it in service to mankind. Offer yourself the benefits of this vital elixir by regularly soaking in a relaxing hot mineral salt bath. A bath infused with minerals, such as magnesium-containing Epsom salts, will relax your muscles and improve your circulation. Salt harmonizes a person's energy field, a benefit for electrically sensitive Aquarians.

★ In addition to Epsom salts, you can also purchase salts derived from the Dead Sea or Himalayan regions, which feature a different mixture of minerals. For additional healing, add flower essences or aromatherapy oils to the bath.

Volunteering

At the heart of an Aquarian's nature is the desire to make a difference, to help better the world. Yet to do so, you don't want to go it alone; rather, as a socially oriented person, you appreciate being part of a collective of like-minded individuals. For an activity that fulfills your altruistic spirit and leaves you feeling more harmonious, consider doing public service work.

★ Volunteering at a food bank, fund-raising for your favorite charity, or advocating for the rights of the underprivileged are just a few of the numerous ways you can contribute to your community, near or far. Look for websites that match your interests, skills, and geographic location to available public service opportunities.

Yoga is a movement practice that lets Aquarians tone their bodies, fortify their life-force energy, and exercise their consciousness.

Downward Facing Dog (*Adho Mukha Svanasana*)

Downward Facing Dog is one of the best poses to bring circulation to the Aquarius-ruled calves and ankles. As you need to focus on many different areas of the body at once during this mild inversion pose, it is particularly well suited to an Aquarian's high level of awareness.

★ Place your hands and knees on the floor, with your wrists slightly in front of your shoulders and your knees below your hips. Spread your fingers wide, and have your middle finger pointing forward. Curl your toes under, and gently push your knees away from the floor, straightening your legs without locking your knees. Lift your sitting bones to the sky, and try to have your heels descend to the floor. Broaden your shoulder blades, and draw them down your back. Your head should rest between your arms. Stay in the pose for up to three minutes.

Noose Pose (*Pashaasana*)

Freedom-loving Aquarians don't generally like restrictions. But the confines of Noose Pose can actually be very liberating to the Water Bearer, because this squatting twist helps stimulate circulation and energy flow, stretch the Achilles tendons, and enhance ankle flexibility.

★ Stand with the right side of your body facing the wall, about a forearm's distance away. Gently twist, placing your right palm on the wall while keeping your forearm parallel to the ground. Bend your knees and slowly move into a squatting position (if your heels don't reach the floor, support them with a folded mat or blanket). Turning your torso to the right, place your left hand on the wall and your left elbow on the outside of the right knee. Press your elbow and knee together, allowing the resistance to help you twist more deeply so that your torso turns to face the wall. Stay in the pose for up to one minute, and then repeat on other side. (For the full expression of the pose, practice without the wall.)

Reclining Big Toe Pose (*Supta Padangusthasana*)

If you want a pose that helps you stretch the back of your legs without placing stress on your lower back, try Reclining Big Toe Pose. It allows you to rest comfortably on the ground, supported by the floor, while you send your leg high into the air, increasing the flexibility of your lower body.

★ Lie on the floor with your legs outstretched. Place a strap around the ball of your right foot. Holding the ends of the strap, gently straighten your leg, sending it toward the ceiling. Flex the right foot while keeping your right hip on the floor. (If you have a lot of flexibility, you can do this posture without the aid of the strap by looping your right index and middle fingers around your big toe.) Your left leg should press into the ground, and your left foot should be flexed. If you need more support, bend the left leg, placing your foot on the floor. Stay in the pose for up to one minute, and repeat on the other side.

AROMATHERAPY

The fragrant smells of essential oils can help progressive and globally focused Water Bearers feel more rooted in their bodies.

Patchouli (*Pogostemon cablin*)

Mirroring the essence of Aquarius, patchouli is one of the scents most associated with the 1960s, conjuring images of that era's free-spiritedness. Yet, its redeeming reputation preceded that; in the early nineteenth century, it was included with shipments of fine Indian fabric imported into Europe, where its scent became a symbol of high quality. Patchouli's sweet musky aroma makes it a grounding aphrodisiac, helping you take root in your body while inspiring openness to sensual pleasure. It is also good for the health of the circulatory system and lower legs.

★ Wear patchouli as a perfume, or bathe in its liberating fragrance. Use it in a room diffuser when you need a bit of grounded uplifting energy. Mix a few drops with some body oil for a tension-freeing and vein-supporting calf massage.

Sweet Marjoram (*Origanum majorana*)

Sweet marjoram is associated with eternal peace and happiness, quintessential Aquarian ideals. This pacifying herb is known for its antispasmodic and circulation-enhancing properties, traditionally used for a variety of cardiovascular concerns including high blood pressure. If your nervous system feels particularly overstimulated, sweet marjoram—with its tension-calming effects—may provide the soothing you need.

★ Place a marjoram-scented sachet under your pillow to help your slumber. If muscle cramps—including those in the Aquarius-ruled calves—have you in a bind, apply marjoram-infused massage oil to your legs.

Benzoin (*Styrax benzoin*)

Burned as incense in the churches and temples of various religions, benzoin is an iconic fragrance signifying spiritual protection. Used in perfumery and healing traditions throughout the world, benzoin is particularly beneficial for Aquarian health in its ability to quiet muscle spasms and support the nervous system. You can also use it for its superior skin-soothing properties.

★ Benzoin is available in a variety of forms including pure resin, essential oil, or powder. Carry a piece of resin with you, inhaling its uplifting fragrance throughout the day. Add a few drops of essential oil to a bath, and enjoy its muscle-relaxing—and numinous—properties.

NATURAL REMEDIES

A trendsetting Aquarian, you probably used natural remedies long before they became popular.

Siberian Ginseng (*Eleutherococcus senticosus*)

Your planetary ruler, Uranus, symbolizes unpredictability. While you are used to expecting the unexpected, even the perceptive Aquarian gets caught off guard by stress and trauma. As an adaptogenic herb, Siberian ginseng can help increase the body's resistance to stresses—whether they be physical, electromagnetic, or chemical—that may otherwise deplete energy. It has also been found to increase mental focus, physical endurance, and immune-system function as well as to protect against stress-related illnesses.

★ Siberian ginseng, also known as *eleuthero*, is available in dried herb, capsule, or liquid tincture form. With its energy-boosting effects, you should not take it close to bedtime. While you can use Siberian ginseng every day, most health-care practitioners recommend a two-week break after using it for two months so the body doesn't become resistant to its effects.

Butcher's Broom (*Ruscus aculeatus*)

If you want to sweep away obstacles that may keep you from optimal health—notably if lower leg health is a concern—try butcher's broom. This saponin-rich herb has been found to be an effective remedy for many people experiencing varicose veins, helping to relieve the leg pain and swelling associated with this condition. Butcher's broom improves sluggish lower-leg circulation by supporting the integrity of the veins as well as combating inflammation.

★ Butcher's broom is available in capsules as well as liquid tincture. Research has found that vitamin C supports the effectiveness of butcher's broom, so consider supplementing with this nutrient as well.

Passionflower (*Passiflora incarnata*)

If you are looking for a natural way to induce calm when your nervous system is overagitated, you might develop a passion for this herbal remedy. You can take passionflower on its own, although it is often found in botanical combination formulas with other sedative herbs, including skullcap and hops. It also comes in a homeopathic version, known as passiflora.

★ Passionflower is available in dried herb, capsule, or liquid tincture form. Mint and coffee can counteract the effectiveness of homeopathic remedies, so avoid them for several hours before and after taking passiflora.

 FLOWER ESSENCES

The fact that a distillation of flowers can deliver psycho-emotional healing doesn't seem odd to an Aquarian, whose out-of-the-box way of thinking allows a greater understanding of the realm of vibrational medicine. All flower essences can be used similarly: mix a few drops in a glass of water, and drink several times a day; add some to a bath; or place in a water-filled mister bottle to enhance your environment.

California Wild Rose (*Rosa californica*)

Abetted by their brilliant minds and progressive vision, Aquarians can be of great service to the world when they are aligned with their ideals. Yet sometimes Water Bearers lose sight of their conviction-filled urns. Veiled in apathy, you might feel more like a spectator of life than a participant. When you need to reenergize your commitment to your ideals, consider using California Wild Rose flower essence.

Dill (*Anethum graveolens*)

While Aquarians respect technology's ability to progress society to a higher level, your enhanced consciousness also makes you more open to feeling its subtle effects in your body. To bolster your aura (your personal electromagnetic field) and avoid short-circuiting your nervous system by stimulation overload, consider Dill flower essence. Think of it as a fusible link, helping protect against excess currents that could overwhelm your individual energy system.

Quaking Grass (*Briza maxima*)

Aquarians are strong individuals who derive much of their identity by belonging to a group. The collective element is important to you because it fosters a much-desired sense of connectivity. Yet feeling at home in a group is not always fun and games, even for the socially minded Aquarian. Quaking Grass flower essence can be used by an individual—as well as members of a group—to help the collective work more harmoniously toward their goals.

pisces

SUN IN PISCES ★ February 19–March 20

CHARACTERISTICS ★ Empathetic / Idealistic / Psychic /
Selfless / Poetic / Absentminded / Spiritual / Impressionable /
Forgiving / Addiction prone / Imaginative / Romantic

SYMBOL ★ A pair of *Fish* bound together yet swimming in
opposite directions, which reflects the mission of integrating
the spiritual and material worlds. In mythological and cultural
traditions, the Fish is a symbol of unity, sacrifice, transformation, and wisdom.

PLANETARY RULER ★ *Neptune*, the planet known for its
oceanic blue color. Neptune was the Roman god of the sea,
who used his trident to both calm and stir the waters. He held
dominion over underwater treasures and mariners' voyages. His
counterpart in Greek mythology was Poseidon. In astrology,
Neptune represents spirituality, transcendence, redemption, and
the imagination.

ELEMENT ★ *Water*, characterized by the fluid energy of emotion, reflection, and nonlinear understanding. It is sensitive,
personal, and responsive.

QUALITY ★ *Mutable*, which represents the adjustment and
finessing stage of the creative cycle. It reflects flexibility, tolerance, and an adaptive and transformative free-flowing force.

The symbol for Pisces—two Fish that are swimming in opposite directions—is a great metaphor for the duality inherent in your sign's attitude toward health. One side of the Piscean nature is characterized by an inclination to ignore messages of *dis*-ease while the other is typified by a tendency to become overly focused on health and well-being issues. Echoing your sign's propensity for paradox, most Pisceans continually float between these two extremes.

The Piscean characteristic of turning a blind eye to health needs reflects your reputation for being the escape artist of the zodiac. As denizens of denial, Pisceans take refuge in daydreams when reality doesn't quite match their idealistic vision of the world. Your dreamy nature often overshadows an ability to feel grounded in, and connected to, your body; as such, you might neglect to notice signs and symptoms of health imbalances. Most Pisceans need to be reminded of the importance of staying rooted in their bodies so that they can be conscious of, rather than overlook, their physical needs.

The Fish's opposite inclination is to obsessively fret on matters of health. A penchant for perfection can make every little itch, bump, or twinge seem like a cause for alarm and a pink slip from good health. Reflecting your sign's dualism, this anxiety-filled focus may cause you to imagine problems where there are none, although it can also echo an innate sensitivity that enables you to perceive what may be imperceptible to many others. The trick, of course, is to readily discern the cause of your hypochondriacal notions, something that can become more clear through relaxation practices such as meditation, which can help you quiet your mind, tune into your body, and align with your inherent Piscean psychic gifts.

Another Piscean characteristic that influences your attitude toward health is a tendency to experience the world in a more holistic and poetic way than others: where many see separation, you see unity. This is one reason that, as a sign, yours ranks high among those most open to natural medicine and mind-body-spirit approaches to healing. When looking for a health-care practitioner, it's best to find one who is extremely compassionate and honors your high level of sensitivity.

 AREAS OF HEALTH FOCUS

Each zodiac sign is associated with certain parts of the body. These may be inherent areas of vulnerability, but when attended to, they can become areas of strength. The parts of the body associated with Pisces include the following:

★ The **feet**, your soulful soles, which connect you to the earth

★ The **immune** and **lymphatic systems**, your body's sentries against infection and disease

★ The **pineal gland**, which synthesizes the hormone melatonin and is associated with the third eye and heightened psychic abilities in several spiritual traditions

Your Piscean psychic abilities, awareness of the mind-body-spirit connection, and innate sense of compassion are some of the resources you can use when facing any health challenge.

Support Your Soulful Soles

Even when walking down the street, Pisceans tend to have their heads in the clouds rather than their focus on the ground, leading to a greater than fair share of stubbed toes. Try to put your inclination to daydream on hold while navigating your environment to avoid running into those couches, curbs, and corners that seem to just magically appear. Also, while you may appreciate the artistic beauty of designer shoes, don't sacrifice comfort for fashion; your gentle soles need support—whether in a strappy sandal or winter boot—to avoid the aches and blisters to which they are inclined. If you are prone to athlete's foot, topically applied tea tree oil may do wonders, as can thoroughly drying your feet after bathing or swimming.

Bolster Your Immune System

Pisceans' wide-eyed nature and fluid personal boundaries make them vulnerable to outside influences. Since bacteria and viruses are no exception, during the change of seasons—or any time you're under undue stress—pay extra attention to bolstering your immune system to protect against colds and flu. To strengthen your defenses, enjoy an array of different nutrient-rich fruits and vegetables throughout the day and consider adding reishi mushrooms, vitamin C, and zinc lozenges to your immune-buoying medicine cabinet. As nervous tension can compromise immune system function, meditation and gentle exercise can help to shore up your permeable boundaries and keep colds and flu at bay.

Get a Good Night's Sleep

As your planetary ruler, Neptune, governs sleep, getting a good night's rest is especially important for Pisceans. It's usually easy for you to dive into slumber the moment your head hits the pillow, but when day-to-day stress rocks your emotional boat, insomnia can become an unwelcome bedfellow. Relaxing essential oils—such as sandalwood and myrrh—and a little evening meditation can be great tools to help you journey to the Land of Nod. Also keep a notebook by your bedside to write down your dreams, a source of great insight for Pisceans and an approach more satisfying than counting sheep should you need assistance falling back to sleep.

Protect Your Vital Energy

While your Piscean intensely caring nature may be one of your greatest gifts, a desire to heal the woes of the world may also be one of your wellness weak spots. You have a tendency to give away a lot of emotional time and space to other people, which can deplete your vital energy reserves and make you more prone to illness. Pisceans hate to see others suffer and sometimes shamanically take on their illnesses; for example, it's not uncommon for you to develop a headache when a friend has one. Don't forget that compassion begins at home: concern for your own wellness—as opposed to solely focusing on everyone else's—will allow you to be an altruist without becoming a martyr. Remember, just because Pisces rules the feet does not mean that you have to walk a mile in everyone's shoes.

HEALTHY EATING TIPS

Often more focused on others than self, Pisceans need to remember that taking the time to nourish their body and spirit through eating well is inextricably linked to well-being.

Eat Consciously

With a tendency to daydream through many of life's activities (including eating), Pisceans can consume a meal in no time flat without even tasting their food or remembering what they ate. Eating consciously is especially beneficial for the Fish, as it can help you feel more grounded in your body.

★ Be mindful when you're eating. Savor your food, taking at least fifteen minutes to enjoy each meal. Chew well and relish each bite, paying attention to its taste, texture, and aroma. Not only will this help you feel more satiated, but it will also lessen your chances of experiencing indigestion. Also, before you eat, say a blessing to honor your food to initiate a mealtime of conscious eating.

Stop Doing the Jitterbug

With your heightened sensitivity, life can often be overwhelming for a Piscean. As a coping mechanism, you might rely on caffeine, sugar, and other substances to bolster your mood and energy level. Yet in reality, this strategy is anything but productive, since your impressionable constitution makes you overly susceptible to their stimulating properties. This can exacerbate feelings of spaciness as well as physical and emotional exhaustion.

★ Think twice before ordering that second latte; instead enjoy rejuvenating, yet caffeine-free, herbal teas such as *rooibos* or *tulsi*. Use agave syrup rather than refined sugar, as it is relatively low on the glycemic index and will have a more stabilizing effect on your blood glucose levels.

Limit the Libations

Enjoying alcoholic beverages is one way that Pisceans temporarily escape experiencing the deluge of feelings that often reside within. Yet, as you know, it only provides a temporary reprieve from emotional woes, not a lasting cure. Plus drowning your sorrows in a sea of Syrah can compromise your liver, leading to reduced energy and immunity. Alcohol is also a diuretic that pulls vital fluid from your body, and therefore, too much is not health-supportive for the water-bound Fish.

★ Slowly drink your beverages to make them go further; this will reduce your alcohol intake and your bar bill. Enjoy one glass of water for each drink you imbibe to stave off dehydration and the chance of experiencing a hangover headache. Have a nonalcoholic "mocktail" instead of a cocktail; teetotaling never tasted so good.

 HEALTH-SUPPORTING FOODS

There are many nutrient-rich foods from the sea that can give you the energy you need to sustain your giving nature while also helping you to feel more grounded, something often challenging for the Fish.

Fish and Shellfish

Not surprisingly, fish and shellfish can play an important role in a healthy Piscean diet. The protein these foods provide gives you long-running energy, while their selenium and zinc help support your immune system. Anti-inflammatory omega-3s—most concentrated in fish such as salmon, sardines, and herring—promote heart health, reduce symptoms of depression, and contribute to radiant skin and hair.

★ Seafood makes a quick and easy dinner, with most types taking less than ten minutes to bake, grill, or poach. A can of high-quality salmon or sardines is an easy-to-pack lunchbox addition that you can readily add to a salad or enjoy as is with a touch of lemon juice and a dash of sea salt.

Sea Vegetables

Other great seafoods for Pisceans are sea vegetables (or seaweed), such as nori, dulse, and kombu. Loaded with minerals—including hard-to-find iodine—sea vegetables make great additions to soups, salads, and, of course, sushi rolls. They also contain polysaccharide phytonutrients that have anti-inflammatory properties.

★ Strips of nori add a spark of phosphorescent color to a green salad. Dulse flakes (available in prepackaged shakers) make a great on-table condiment. Add kombu when cooking a pot of beans to guard against legume-related flatulence. To reduce your exposure to heavy metals, buy sea vegetables from high-quality manufacturers who routinely test their products.

Sea Salt

If you are going to add salt to your meals, consider using sea salt instead of regular table salt. Derived from evaporated seawater rather than land-based halite deposits, mineral-rich sea salt aligns energetically with the Piscean's aqueous constitution. Different types of sea salt feature distinctive flavors, from pure and simple to richly oceanic.

★ Experiment with many varieties of sea salt as each features a different color, texture, and taste. Some interesting ones include French *fleur-de-sel*, pink-colored Hawaiian, and pyramid-shaped Balinese sea salt. Just be careful not to go overboard with your salt intake, which can lead to swelling, especially in those sensitive Piscean feet.

 SPA AND WELLNESS THERAPIES

If you feel like escaping from the world, head for a spa, where you can enjoy treatments that will soothe your mind and nurture your body.

Hypnotherapy

Since Pisceans are especially open to the thoughts and feelings that reside in their subconscious, hypnotherapy—which facilitates access to this part of the mind—may be an especially effective wellness modality for the Fish. Hypnotherapy is particularly good for reducing chronic pain, counteracting anxiety and insomnia, and alleviating stress-related illnesses. It can also be helpful for releasing addictive behaviors, something with which sensitive Pisceans may struggle.

★ To learn more about hypnotherapy and find practitioners in your area, visit the websites of the American Society of Clinical Hypnosis (www.asch.net) and the National Board for Certified Clinical Hypnotherapists (www.natboard.com).

Reflexology

Reflexology, a form of bodywork focused almost exclusively on the feet, seems custom-made for Pisceans. A reflexology practitioner reads the feet like a map of the body and applies pressure to the areas corresponding to the body parts that need some extra attention. More than just a simple foot massage, reflexology seeks to reduce imbalances in the body by stimulating specific nerves and energy channels in the feet.

★ Most reflexologists are also massage therapists, chiropractors, or podiatrists. Natural health stores sell pocket-sized reflexology maps, allowing you to practice this healing practice as part of your self-care regimen.

Watsu

Because Pisceans are generally at home in the water, Watsu, a form of aquatic bodywork, is well suited to the Fish. During a

Watsu session, you float in a pool of warm water while the practitioner gently sways and stretches your body. Being suspended in water is not only soothing, but it also allows your body to be moved in ways that would be impossible on a massage table. Watsu helps to relax your muscles, realign your energy, and calm your mind, providing moments of meditative bliss, a cherished haven for spiritually inclined Pisceans.

★ Waterdance is a type of aquatic bodywork similar to Watsu, although it involves being lowered under the water's surface. The Worldwide Aquatic Bodywork Association offers a practitioner directory on their website (www.waba.edu).

RELAXATION PRACTICES

Taking the time to relax, participating in mind-centering activities, and connecting with the deeper parts of your self can do wonders for a Piscean's sense of well-being.

Meditation

Meditation helps to calm the churning seas of the mind, body, and spirit. Being still, even for twenty minutes a day, can help you align with the deeper parts of yourself, which is very important for a soul-searching Piscean. In addition to helping you connect with your core, meditation has many well-documented health benefits; it reduces stress-related illnesses, combats insomnia, and improves heart health.

★ While there are a variety of different meditation techniques, mindfulness meditation, breath meditation, and transcendental meditation (or TM) are among the most popular. To find the one most aligned with your personal needs, explore the many books, CDs, and classes available on these different practices.

Swimming

As you might have guessed, swimming is one of the best forms of exercise for a Piscean. It helps you unwind as you fluidly move your body through the water. Swimming provides a cardiovascular workout that's gentle and low impact, perfect for your sensitive temperament. If you don't have access to a pool—or lake, stream, or ocean—soaking in a bathtub can do wonders to release tension on both a physical and emotional level.

★ Many colleges and community centers offer swimming courses geared toward a variety of levels. Lighting candles, playing soft music, and adding fragrant essential oils to the tub can transform a regular bath into a soulfully relaxing experience.

Walking

Walking is a gentle form of exercise that allows your Piscean feet to connect to the Earth. Not only will a peaceful promenade calm the mind but walking also provides the added benefit of stimulating your lymphatic system and strengthening your immunity. Just make sure to wear supportive shoes when out for a walk so that a potentially relaxing experience doesn't transform itself into one spent worrying about your aching feet.

★ As an added Piscean treat, incorporate water into this relaxation practice. For example, after a walk, soak your feet in a footbath infused with sea salt to relax your soles and enliven your spirit.

Pisceans like to get lost in the sea of their thoughts and feelings, and yoga is a constructive way to do so as it is a moving meditation that fosters a connection to body, mind, and spirit.

Child's Pose (*Balasana*)

Child's Pose stretches and massages the feet. Yogis also say that it helps to stimulate the third eye, the seat of Piscean psychic abilities.

★ Kneel on the floor with your knees together and the tops of your feet on the floor (for wide-style Child's Pose, spread your knees a little wider than the distance of your hips). Rest your buttocks on your heels, and bend forward until your torso rests on your thighs and your forehead on the floor. Your arms can either be extended out straight in front of you or to your sides with your palms next to your feet. Stay in the pose for as long as needed to feel rejuvenated.

Fish Pose (*Matsyasana*)

Fish Pose helps open both the heart chakra—connecting you to feelings of love—and the throat chakra—helping you more fluidly communicate these radiant feelings.

★ Lie on your back with your legs outstretched. With your palms on the floor, place your hands under your buttocks. Your forearms will be angled out to the side. On an inhalation, gently lift your torso, and move your forearms so they are in the same line as your torso (this will cause your upper arms to ascend from the floor). Arching your middle back, tilt your head backward so the crown of your head comes to the floor. Stay in the pose for up to thirty seconds. To come out of the pose, press your forearms into the ground, and on an exhale, gently release your head and lay it on the floor, moving your arms beside your torso.

Toe Crunch Pose

This descriptively named pose may not have a Sanskrit moniker, but that doesn't detract from the authentic benefits that it can provide. Toe Crunch Pose is one of the best postures when it comes to circulating energy to your feet.

★ Kneel on the floor with your knees together and your toes curled under (so the bottoms of your feet are at an angle to the floor rather than touching it). Start off leaning forward with your hands gently resting on the floor in front of your knees. You should feel your toes and the balls of your feet opening up. Slowly move toward sitting back on your heels, with your torso vertical (or until the point where it gets uncomfortable); this will intensify the stretch. Stay in the pose for up to one minute.

AROMATHERAPY

Essential oils provide Pisceans with an exquisitely effective way to lift their spirits and connect with their innate psychic and artistic talents.

Sandalwood (*Santalum album* and *S. spicatum*)

Sandalwood oil is derived from the fragrant wood of the sandalwood tree. The smell of sandalwood is said to heighten the ability to make connections between the seen and unseen, a useful tool to aid in Piscean artistry. It is thought to energize the pineal gland—and by association, psychic gifts. Sandalwood also helps quell nervous tension and depression, and it has aphrodisiac properties.

★ Dab some sandalwood oil in the center of your forehead to enhance your intuition. Inspire romanticism by misting sandalwood-infused water onto your bed linens. Wear a *japa mala,* a string of Tibetan prayer beads made from sandalwood, so this mystic scent can guide you throughout the day.

Myrrh (*Commiphera myrrha*)

Myrrh has been revered for its sacred properties throughout history. It figures prominently in the Bible—being one of the gifts of the magi—as well as ancient Egyptian texts. Throughout the world, myrrh has been used as incense in holy temples. It has divine skin-care properties as well, great for healing wounds, soothing dry skin, and mollifying heel fissures.

★ When you want a spirit-lifting aroma or an aid to your meditation practice, consider using myrrh in a diffuser to scent a room. Massage your feet with myrrh-scented body lotion to allay dry skin and heal cracked heels.

Tea Tree Oil (*Melaleuca alternifolia*)

When it comes to warding off infections and buoying the Pisces-ruled immune system, tea tree oil is in a class all its own. Its antiseptic properties are widespread, having antibacterial, antiviral, *and* antifungal activities. Yet its benefits are not limited to the physical: the smell of tea tree oil has mood-elevating properties and inspires feelings of optimism.

★ As tea tree oil can help with athlete's foot, mix some with an unscented body cream and use as needed. If dandruff or dry scalp is a problem, add a few drops to your shampoo. Use some in a steam inhalation when a respiratory illness has you down.

NATURAL REMEDIES

Herbs, dietary supplements, and homeopathics are natural ways for Pisceans to fortify their physical boundaries.

Reishi Mushrooms (*Ganoderma lucidum*)

As your planetary ruler, Neptune, is traditionally associated with mushrooms, it makes sense that reishi mushrooms (known as *Lingzhi* in Chinese) would be a top pick when it comes to an herbal supplement for the Fish. Used in traditional Chinese medicine for more than two thousand years, *Lingzhi* means "herb of spiritual potency," perfect for the soulful Piscean. Reishi is one of the premier adaptogens, a class of herbs that enhance the body's resistance to stress and fatigue, bolstering the immune system.

★ Reishi mushrooms are available in various forms including capsules, powder, liquid tincture, and tea. Reishi is often combined with maitake mushrooms in dietary supplements.

Fish Oil

If you cannot eat omega-3–rich fish—such as salmon, sardines, or herring—several times a week, you may want to consider taking fish oil supplements. The "good" fats contained in fish oil have anti-inflammatory properties and are a great boon to wellness: they lower cholesterol, lubricate joints, and enhance skin and hair health. People who experience depression—something to which sensitive Pisceans are vulnerable—are often deficient in this important nutrient.

★ Look for fish-oil products from manufacturers that use third-party testing to ensure that their products are free of polychlorinated biphenyls (PCBs), heavy metals, and other contaminants. Pisceans looking for a vegetarian source of omega-3s may want to consider flaxseed oil and/or algae supplements.

Homeopathic Phosphorus

Different homeopathic remedies are associated with different psychological constitutions; the one affiliated with homeopathic phosphorus is well matched to the Piscean archetype, that of a person with very fluid boundaries who can absorb the thoughts and feelings of others. It is also a good remedy for nervous tension, insomnia, dizziness, and headaches that are exacerbated by warm weather.

★ Low-dose phosphorus is available in health food stores and natural pharmacies. Higher-dose forms, which work better as constitutional remedies, are best taken under the guidance of a homeopathic physician. Mint and coffee can counteract the effectiveness of homeopathic remedies, so avoid them for several hours before and after taking phosphorus.

 FLOWER ESSENCES

There's an innate poetry to flower essences—vibrational elixirs that provide attunement to different levels of emotional imbalance—that deeply resonates with a Piscean. All flower essences can be used similarly: mix a few drops in a glass of water, and drink several times a day; add some to a bath; or place in a water-filled mister bottle to enhance your environment.

Nicotiana (*Nicotiana alata*)

That expansive empathetic nature can sometimes make Pisceans feel like they are drowning in a sea of emotion. In response, many turn to substances (such as tobacco and alcohol) or activities (such as shopping and watching television) through which they can temporarily escape the realities of the world—and the deluge of feelings they can engender in the Fish. Instead, try Nicotiana flower essence: it can fortify your heart, giving you a flotation aid with which to ride the emotional waves rather than feel submerged by them.

Aspen (*Populus tremula*)

Known as the "psychic sponge" of the zodiac, Pisceans innately pick up on the thoughts and feelings of others. Yet if you absorb these without discernment, it can lead to confusion ("is this my feeling or someone else's?") or low-level anxiety (especially if the feelings that come to you are mired in fear). Aspen flower essence helps to calm the mind, allowing you to better sift through the impressions you receive. This can help you discriminate among those that swim within you so you don't take on others' emotions and negativity as if they were your own.

Pink Yarrow (*Achillea millefolium* var. *rubra*)

The Fish tends to overidentify with the suffering of others. While your compassionate nature is one of your virtues, if you give away too much of yourself, it can lead to a slow leak in vital energy. This drain in your energetic resources, combined with your inclination to merge emotionally with others, can make you vulnerable to psychosomatic illness and depressive tendencies. Pink Yarrow flower essence strengthens your fluid personal boundaries, helping you gain objectivity while still maintaining your empathetic spirit. This way you can be compassionate without losing your center, or yourself.

RESOURCES

You can learn about astrology and natural health topics from a vast array of resources. Here are some of my favorites:

Astrology

Arroyo, Stephen. *Astrology, Karma, and Transformation: The Inner Dimensions of the Birth Chart.* Sebastopol, CA: CRCS Publications, 1992.

Baum, Laurie A. *Everything You Need to Know about Your Astrology Sign.* Bloomington, IN: iUniverse, Inc., 2007.

Hand, Robert. *Horoscope Symbols.* West Chester, PA: Whitford Press, 1981.

Hickey, Isabel M. *Astrology: A Cosmic Science.* Sebastopol, CA: CRCS Publications, 1992.

The Mountain Astrologer magazine (www.mountainastrologer.com).

Sakoian, Frances, and Acker, Louis S. *The Astrologer's Handbook.* New York, NY: Harper Perennial, 1989.

Tarnas, Richard. *Cosmos and Psyche: Intimations of a New World View.* New York, NY: Plume, 2007.

Woolfolk, Joanna Martine. *The Only Astrology Book You'll Ever Need.* Lanham, MD: Taylor Trade Publishing, 2008.

Medical Astrology

Cornell, Howard Leslie. *Encyclopaedia of Medical Astrology.* St. Paul, MN: Llewellyn Publications, 1972.

Culpeper, Nicholas. *Astrological Judgement of Diseases from the Decumbiture of the Sick.* Bel Air, MD: Astrology Classics, 2003.

———. *Culpeper's Complete Herbal.* London: Wordsworth Editions, 1995.

Däath, Heinrich. *Medical Astrology.* New York, NY: Cosimo Classics, 2005.

Ebertin, Reinhold. *Astrological Healing.* York Beach, ME: Samuel Weiser, 1989.

Jansky, Robert Carl. *Astrology, Nutrition & Health.* Atglen, PA: Whitford Press, 1977.

Nauman, Eileen. *Medical Astrology.* Cottonwood, AZ: Blue Turtle Publishing, 1982.

Ridder-Patrick, Jane. *A Handbook of Medical Astrology*. Edinburgh, Scotland: CrabApple Press, 2006.

Starck, Marcia. *Healing with Astrology*. Freedom, CA: Crossing Press, 1997.

Diet, Nutrition, and Health

Haas, Elson M., and Levin, Buck. *Staying Healthy with the Seasons*. Berkeley, CA: Celestial Arts, 2006.

Lad, Vasant. *The Complete Book of Ayurvedic Home Remedies*. New York, NY: Three Rivers Press, 1999.

Mateljan, George. *The World's Healthiest Foods: Essential Guide for the Healthiest Way of Eating*. Seattle, WA: GMF Publishing, 2007.

Nestle, Marion. *What to Eat*. New York, NY: North Point Press, 2006.

Pitchford, Paul. *Healing with Whole Foods*. Berkeley, CA: North Atlantic Books, 2002.

Planck, Nina. *Real Food: What to Eat and Why*. New York, NY: Bloomsbury USA, 2007.

Pollan, Michael. *In Defense of Food: An Eater's Manifesto*. New York, NY: Penguin Press, 2008.

Wood, Rebecca. *The New Whole Foods Encyclopedia: A Comprehensive Resource for Healthy Eating*. New York, NY: Penguin Compass, 1999.

Yoga

Desikachar, T. K. V. *The Heart of Yoga: Developing a Personal Practice*. Rochester, VT: Inner Traditions, 1999.

Iyengar, B. K. S. *Light on Yoga: The Bible of Modern Yoga*. New York, NY: Schocken, 1995.

Meza, Melina. *Art of Sequencing*. Seattle, WA: Melina Meza Press, 2007.

Aromatherapy

Mojay, Gabriel. *Aromatherapy for Healing the Spirit*. Rochester, VT: Healing Arts Press, 2000.

Ryman, Daniele. *The Aromatherapy Bible*. London, England: Piatkus, 1991.

Schaubelt, Kurt. *Advanced Aromatherapy*. Rochester, VT: Healing Arts Press, 1998.

Valnet, Jean. *The Practice of Aromatherapy*. Rochester, NY: Healing Arts Press, 1982.

Natural Remedies

Gerber, Richard. *Vibrational Medicine*. Rochester, VT: Bear & Company, 2001.

Grieve, M. *A Modern Herbal*. New York, NY: Dover, 1971.

Murray, Michael, and Pizzorno, Joseph. *Encyclopedia of Natural Medicine*. New York, NY: Three Rivers Press, 1997.

Patnaik, Naveen. *The Garden of Life: An Introduction to the Healing Plants of India*. New York, NY: Aquarian, 1993.

Tierra, Michael. *The Way of Herbs*. New York, NY: Pocket, 1998.

Flower Essences

Craydon, Deborah, and Bellows, Warren. *Floral Acupuncture*. Berkeley, CA: Crossing Press, 2005.

Damian, Peter. *Astrological Study of the Bach Flower Essences*. York Beach, ME: Samuel Weiser, 1986.

Kaminski, Patricia, and Katz, Richard. *Flower Essence Repertory*. Nevada City, CA: Flower Essence Society, 1994.

Websites: How to Find an Astrologer

American Federation of Astrologers
www.astrologers.com

International Society for Astrological Research
www.isarastrology.com

National Council for Geocosmic Research
www.geocosmic.org

Organization for Professional Astrology
www.professional-astrology.org

Websites: Astrology and Horoscopes

Astro.com
Offers horoscope reports as well as a free service through which you can cast your personal astrology chart and find your Accendant and Moon signs

PlanetaryApothecary.com

Provides ongoing exploration of wellness and astrology topics, and features resources where you can learn more about your personal astrological profile

StarIQ.com

Features a personal-horoscope email service plus articles about numerous astrology-related topics

INDEX

ABOUT THE AUTHOR

 **STEPHANIE GAILING**, MS, CN, is a professional nutritionist and astrologer with more than sixteen years of experience. She has covered whole foods, herbs, dietary supplements, yoga, and astrology for numerous publications. For the past nine years, Stephanie has been a consultant to the World's Healthiest Foods website (www.whfoods.org). In addition to writing and editing, Stephanie's career in the natural health field includes operating her own eco-products retail store and serving as a nutrition education consultant for companies in the natural products industry. She holds a master's degree in nutrition from Bastyr University and is a certified nutritionist in Washington State. She lives in Seattle.